Poor Super Man

The cast of the Edmonton production of *Poor Super Man. Left to right:* Ian Leung, Kate Ryan, Christopher Peterson, Kent Staines, Jill Dyck. *Photo: Kristina Hahn*

POOR SUPER MAN

A Play
With Captions

# Brad Fraser

NeWest Press
Edmonton

Prairie Play Series: 14 / Series Editor, Diane Bessai

Canadian Cataloguing in Publication Data

Fraser, Brad, 1959-
    Poor Super Man

    (Prairie play series ; 14)
    ISBN 0-920897-81-9

    I. Title. II. Series.
    PS8561.R294P6 1995    C812'.54    C95-910075-X
    PR9199.3F72P6 1995

Board Editor: Diane Bessai
Editor: Don Perkins
Editorial Coordinator: Eva Radford
Cover design: Brian Huffman
Cover art: Based on a poster design by Brad Fraser and Darrin Hagen
Book design: Brenda Burgess

NeWest Press gratefully acknowledges the financial assistance of The Canada Council; The Alberta Foundation for the Arts, a beneficiary of the Lottery Fund of the Government of Alberta; and The NeWest Institute for Western Canadian Studies.

Photographs have been reproduced with the kind permission of the following: The Ensemble Theatre of Cincinnati, photos by Sandy Underwood; Sean Hudson, Edinburgh; Workshop West/Theatre Network, photos by Kristina Hahn and Ed Ellis.

"The Transmutation" by Steven Dyson reprinted by permission of the author. Excerpt from *Shift Magazine* reprinted by permission of the publisher.

Printed and bound in Canada

NeWest Publishers Limited
Suite 310, 10359 - 82 Avenue / Edmonton, Alberta T6E 1Z9

For Jeffrey Hirschfield,


Paul Reynolds,


and Hank VanSteenwyk

## The Transmutation

I stand glibly
on the other side
of reality
watching a fire burn
feverishly
out of control
and I do not care
even as I hear
familiar voices
screaming and pleading
for help
I am frozen
I am . . .
far too rapt
in the wonder
of how
I could have drowned
in someone
so shallow
as you

Oh is this how it feels
to live in a reality
to die
in a dream

Silently
like a liar
stealing
a secret
I cross the line
through the smoke
the fire
and travel
to a place
where only embers
long
for the treachery
of the flame
to a place
where promises
flatter the flaws
which lurk
in the wreckage
of assimilation
to a place
where suddenly . . .
my name
is nobody

— Steven Dyson  1987

Brad Fraser plays published by NeWest Press:

*The Wolf Plays*, including *Wolfboy*
and *Prom Night of the Living Dead*
Prairie Play Series: Number 12

*The Ugly Man*
Prairie Play Series: Number 13

# Contents

# Introduction

This is what happened.

I was freshly returned to Toronto from L.A. where I had met with a number of studio executives who had seen the script I wrote for the Denys Arcand film, *Love and Human Remains*. They wanted to talk to me about future projects. The meetings had gone well and I flew back into the frozen North feeling rather good about my work and the future in general.

The telephone rang. It was my agent. He was calling to tell me that my latest play, *Poor Super Man*, had just been postponed in Cincinnati, where it was scheduled to have its premier production in April of 1994.

Postponed? What did that mean? My agent had been given some vague line about "a possible future date." Essentially, the Ensemble Theatre of Cincinnati — which bills itself as Cincinnati's "alternate" theatre — felt the content of the play was too controversial for them to produce. They had decided to cancel the show in order not to alienate their subscription audience or jeopardize future funding possibilities. Translation: they were cancelling the show — despite the fact contracts had already been signed and my guarantee had been paid.

This — or something like this — always happens. To me anyway.

When my first play, *Mutants*, was done at Walterdale Theatre in Edmonton, the board of directors balked at producing the show two days before auditions were to happen because they felt the material was too "raw." Thankfully, a number of high-powered board members interceded on my behalf and the show went ahead.

When I was writing *Wolfboy*, the director of the initial production convinced me to change the ending because he felt it would be "hard for the audience to relate to all the fucking and sucking." Being new to the theatre and not wanting to piss anyone off quite yet, I changed the ending.

At the Alberta Theatre Projects playRites! Festival, *Unidentified Human Remains and the True Nature of Love* was almost killed before it'd been seen when a group of terrified actors, a nervous theatre, and a director quit a week before the opening.

Why do theatres — and particularly boards of directors of theatres — react so strongly to the work? The most obvious answer is, of course, HOMOPHOBIA.

Being a homosexual, my work quite naturally includes a great deal of overt homosexual content. Men fall in love and have sex with other men. Women get involved with other women. Cocks are sucked. Asses are fucked. Vaginas are licked and fingered. People have sex. All kinds of sex. I find it impossible to write about relationships without including sex. It seems unrealistic and irresponsible.

I am aware that many people are uncomfortable with sexual behaviour, particularly homosexual behaviour.

Especially in America where straight white men prefer to keep all gay contact in the dark where they can indulge without their wives finding out about it. This fear is clearly seen in the military debate that proves, beyond a shadow of a doubt, that straight men are afraid of natural interaction with homosexuals because of the sexual tension that might be aroused. Sexual tension cannot exist with only one party contemplating the act.

I also know many straight people are threatened by the gay community and the inevitable juggernaut the gay movement for equal rights has become. After all, gays as a group are not only better educated, better built, better informed, better paid, and more articulate than the average straight person — we also have better sex, better taste, and are almost exclusively responsible for anything beautiful that has ever been created by humankind. Of course they want to shut us up and hide us away.

However, one has to be careful with the charge of homophobia. It is a term bandied about far too easily. And, although the theatre is far from perfect, it is one of the few contemporary entertainment media where gays have been able to tell their stories in their own distinctive voices. In fact, the theatre is one place where gay voices seem not only to exist, but to thrive. Certainly a quick survey leading to names such as Tennessee Williams, Edward Albee, Mark Crowley, Martin Sherman, Brydon McDonald, Michel Tremblay, Daniel MacIvor, and many others would indicate that gay men, at least, are able to establish themselves in the theatre. And certainly many of these writers have explored territory every bit as risqué and daring as anything I've done.

This is what I think.

I think the problem with my work and some people's reaction to it, while encompassing certain homophobic attitudes, is actually something else. I think the real problem is ACTION. Physical action. Sexual action. Violent action. Dramatic action.

Based on a tired model foisted on us by a lot of second rate, expatriate, British taxidermists who try to pass off what they do as directing (most of whom run our major regionals into the ground), the Canadian theatre has become a very rarefied place. Action and narrative have been sacrificed for character, metaphor, and debate. Fine. If that's what you're into there's plenty of it to be found. It's not what I'm into.

I want to create and attend a theatre that speaks the vocabulary I use day to day. Not the one I inherited second rate from our inbred English cousins or less-than-sophisticated American neighbours. This is not to say that I'm not interested in exploring multifaceted issues or complex characters. Quite the opposite. That's exactly what I want to do. But I want to do it through what the characters DO, no just what they say and think. I grew up watching naturalistic theatre with one set and four characters, all of whom talk about things that happened in the past until they are led to some sort of internal character revelation. Frankly, nine times out of ten, it's a huge yawn.

Film, television, music, video, comic books, and computers have changed the way we think, the way we see, and the way we absorb information. We have no need to be told stories in the same way our parents were — or their parents were. We need to reinvent the theatre to serve our own purposes — and we need to do it in a language

that engages not only us — but also those other genera-
tions behind us who share our post-1969 television
vocabulary. We need to draw a new audience into the
theatre and show them why it's exciting.

At least that's my opinion.

A lot of people working within the theatre disagree with
me. A lot of the members of the boards of directors sup-
porting theatres disagree with me. That's fine. I disagree
with what they think theatre should be as well. I guess
the difference is, I don't try to shut them down. I don't try
to ban their plays. I don't interfere with their right to be
produced or to speak out or air their opinions.

Instead, I react with my work. Rather than wasting a
monumental amount of time and energy trying to shut
them up, I simply write the plays that carry my ideas
and, hopefully, prove my points.

*Poor Super Man* was reinstated in its allotted seasonal
slot in Cincinnati. The threat of legal action and public
embarrassment as well as the unwavering support of the
artists at the Ensemble Theater of Cincinnati caused the
board to reconsider their decision to cancel the show. It
opened as planned.

And, more than likely, when the next play I write is sent
out to whatever theatre decides to produce it, the board
of directors will read the script, worry that it's going to
alienate the subscription audience and various funding
bodies, and attempt to cancel the show. It will open as
planned.

At that point, I will start the battle that I've had to fight

every time a show is produced. I will charge homophobia. I will threaten legal action. I will enlist the support
of my fellow artists. I will pull out reviews and box office
reports for all my other plays in order to justify their
existence. I will do everything within my power to be
granted the same rights and considerations as anyone
else. I will, as I have in the past, expend huge amounts of
time and energy working to convince the very people
who are supposed to be sympathetic to what I am
attempting to do, not to censor and silence me. And I will
fight the same battle each and every time. Because it's a
battle worth fighting.

— Brad Fraser
Reprinted from *Shift Magazine* (Spring 1994)

Poor Super Man was developed as part of the Canadian Stage Play Creation Unit in May of 1993. It received three subsequent workshops, also at the Canadian Stage, in June, July, and October of 1993. The following artists were involved in the workshops: Nancy Beatty, John Devorski, Andrew Dolha, Allegra Fulton, Gale Garnett, Paulina Gillis, Brian Hill, Daniel MacIvor, Michael Mahonen, Vickie Papavs, Carol Sinclair, and Kent Staines.

Also acknowledged are Bob Baker, Candace Burley, Derek Goldby, and Iris Turcotte.

### First Performance

The premier of Poor Super Man was produced by Ensemble Theatre of Cincinnati, 27 April – 15 May 1994, under the direction of Mark Mocahbee.

### Cast:

David   *Michael J. Blankenship*
Matt   *Damian Baldet*
Shannon   *David Schaplowsky*
Kryla   *Annie Fitzpatrick*
Violet   *Shannon Rae Lutz*

Assistant Director   *Jasson Minadakis*
Scenic and Costume Designer   *Ronald A. Shaw*
Composer/Original Music   *Darrin Hagen*
Lighting Designer   *James H. Gage*

The European premier of Poor Super Man was produced by Traverse Theatre, Edinburgh, 15 July – 7 August 1994 and for the Edinburgh Festival 16 August – 3 September, under the direction of Ian Brown. This production transferred to the Hampstead Theatre, London, 15 September – 15 October 1994.

**Cast:**

David  *Ian Gelder*
Matt  *Christopher Simon*
Shannon  *Jude Akuwudike*
Kryla  *Elaine Collins*
Violet  *Kathryn Howden*

Assistant Director  *Deborah Yhip*
Designer  *Tim Hatley*
Sound Designer  *John Irvine*
Lighting Designer  *Ian Sommerville*


The Canadian premier was co-produced by Workshop West and Theatre Network, Edmonton, October 13 – 30, 1994, under the direction of Brad Fraser.

**Cast:**

David  *Kent Staines*
Matt  *Ian Leung*
Shannon  *Christopher Peterson*
Kryla  *Jill Dyck*
Violet  *Kate Ryan*

Assistant Director/Slide Operator  *Heather D. Swain*
Design Coordinator  *David Skelton*
Costume Designer  *Dave Boechler*
Lighting Design  *Judith Bowden*
Composer  *Darrin Hagen*

# A Play With Captions

## Brad Fraser

**Characters:**

David, a man
Matt, a man
Shannon, a man turning into a woman
Kryla, a woman
Violet, a woman

**Setting:**

Calgary, Alberta, Canada. Various locations. Mostly David's studio and the Monteray Diner.

**Production Notes:**

*Poor Super Man* is a play with captions. It may be advantageous to find a multitude of places to project the captions, including the back wall, the floor, the ceiling, and even the actors' chests or faces.

The captions serve a variety of purposes — from the practical (*setting, time*, etc.) to the more impressionistic. Some of the captions are meant to do nothing more than evoke a vague feeling or image or reflect an inner voice for a particular character.

These captions, along with the sound effects, any musical accompaniment, and the spoken text, are meant to form a continuous, nonstop barrage of information that will create a theatrical equivalent of the information we are inundated with in everyday life. The captions should fade in and out of the dialogue and action in a manner that reflects and in some ways controls the pace of the show.

The captions are placed where a pause would normally exist in the text. The captions should fill the pauses found by the actors and director in the rhythms of the play. The way the captions are seen should vary. Some may be quick, some slow, some pulse, some flash, some fade up and fade down. The more varied they are the better they work. No points in the play should exist where there are breaks between lines without a visual caption to accompany them, unless it is indicated in the script with the word *Pause*.

This play is meant to flow swiftly. Any costume changes, set changes, entrances, exits, etc. should happen only if they do not impede the pace and drive of the show.

This work is not structured like more conventional forms of theatre and cannot be acted like other plays. There is very little time to build into a particular emotional or intellectual state. The actors must be able to access their emotional reality instantly and change that reality on command. Actors should be encouraged to take as much time as they need for the delivery of the line, but must not take that time *between* the lines. The words of the play are never reflective and they are never inactive. They are always moving forward for some purpose involving the other characters in the play. None of the characters enters having made an offstage decision. All decisions are found in the text. There are no blackouts in the show. All stage directions happen *with* the dialogue, not between it. Mood and atmosphere are established *with* the dialogue and action, not around it. These characters are all very comfortable with the language they speak.

Parenthetical information is for the actors and director. It is not meant to be spoken or used in captions.

*Darkness. Credits flash on the back wall of the stage as the opening music is heard. The music fades as the credits end. The captions flash very quickly through the following sequence.*

**Caption run:**   Men Art Women Love Life Love Women Art Men

**Caption:**   Men

*A light on Matt.*

**Matt:**   It's like I know how I feel — what I want to say — inside, but I don't know how to get it out.

**Caption:**   Art

*Light on David.*

**David:**   It's about colour. The individual colours none of us see in quite the same tone or intensity.

**Caption:**   Women

*A light rises on Kryla.*

**Kryla:**   Two things in the world I know for sure. If you dye your hair once you'll never stop and if you're born with a cunt you're fucked.

**Caption:**   Love

*A light rises on Violet.*

**Violet:** It's like we're all speaking different languages and we only understand every third or fourth word.

**Caption:** Life

*A light rises on Shannon.*

**Shannon:** I've always thought a vagina was the true test. Anyone can buy breasts.

**Caption:** His Studio Day

*David stands before a large blank canvas supported on a tech metal easel. David moves as if to draw on the canvas with charcoal. Halfway to the canvas his arm drops. He turns away from the canvas with disgust.*

**Caption:** Empty

*David goes to his drug box and takes out a joint. He sits in the large windowledge. Shannon enters.*

**Shannon:** Hairball. *[a greeting]*

**David:** Fishbag. *[a greeting]*

**Shannon:** Date with my psychologist.

**David:** Nervous?

**Shannon:** *Nods.* There's a box riding on this visit.

**David:** Good luck.

**Shannon:** I'm ready ready ready.

**David:** How're you feeling?

**Shannon:** Fine. What're you painting?

**David:**   Nothing.

**Shannon:**   You feeling Jean Tierney? *[weird]*

**David:**   Totally Tierney.

**Shannon:**   Want an Ativan?

**David:**   Let's smoke a joint?

**Shannon:**   This is a psychological evaluation. I have to be straight.

**David:**   You're hardly straight on Ativan.

**Shannon:**   Ativan's legal.

*David lights the joint and holds it out to Shannon.*

**Shannon:**   No.

**David:**   Whatta Teresa. *[chickenshit]*

**Shannon:**   Paint something.

**David:**   Can't.

**Shannon:**   Why not?

**David:**   I don't know. Nothing comes.

**Shannon:**   Paint what you know.

**David:**   Gallery openings and interviewers? Please.

**Shannon:**   Paint me.

**David:**   Nude? Dick and all?

**Shannon:** The dick's not mine.

**David:** Hideous mistake.

**Shannon:** Absolutely.

**David:** Nearly finished this joint.

**Shannon:** Naw. I wanna be straight for Dr. Whozit. I've gotta take the C Train . . .

**David:** *Cutting Shannon off.* He's not gonna do it.

**Caption:** Scalpel

**David:** It's surgery. Your immune system won't be able to handle it. They cut your dink off. They cut it off. And then they cut a huge hole between your legs and they line the hole with the chickenskin from your knob — only it's not as sensitive . . .

**Shannon:** *Cutting him off.* I know what the operation involves.

**David:** I saw one done.

**Shannon:** Where?

**David:** Shocking Asia.

**Shannon:** What's that?

**David:** This vid. It was hid. *[hideous]* Showed them cutting this guy's wiener off.

**Shannon:** You're not awake for it.

**David:** They won't do it when you have AIDS.

**Caption:**   Incision

**Shannon:**   I have to have this operation.

**David:**   It's thousands of dollars.

**Shannon:**   I have to be a woman.

**David:**   I just don't want you to be disappointed.

**Shannon:**   What's made you so mean?

**Caption:**   Loneliness

**David:**   I didn't say it to be mean.

**Shannon:**   You said it because you're having trouble
painting.

**David:**   I said it because you're not being realistic.

**Shannon:**   Realistic's boring darling.

**David:**   Everything's boring darling.

**Shannon:**   Jaded.

**David:**   Cranky.

**Shannon:**   Can I borrow the car?

**David:**   Snatchurally.

*David tosses keys to Shannon.*

**Shannon:**   Thanks babe.

**David:**   Shut up fuck you.

**Shannon:**  Love ya. Mean it.

*Shannon exits. David gives the empty canvas a dark glance and paces.*

**Caption:**  Goodbye Trixie

*The restaurant. Matt is loading milk into the bar fridge. Violet enters.*

**Violet:**  We owe the garbage people money and the liquor order's too big.

**Matt:**  I don't think Trixie's gonna work out.

**Violet:**  Too slow for a second waiter anyway.

**Matt:**  We need one for that five o'clock rush. If Trixie gets two tables at the same time she's in the shit.

**Violet:**  Put an ad in the paper tomorrow.

**Matt:**  Another fifty bucks.

**Violet:**  Jesus. Y'can't leave the house without it costing fifty bucks.

**Matt:**  Guess I'll have to fire her after her shift.

**Violet:**  Okay with that?

**Matt:**  She thinks I hate her.

**Violet:**  Do you?

**Matt:**  She's a really bad waiter.

**Violet:**  I'll do it.

**Matt:** You sure?

**Violet:** I'll just tell her we can't afford to keep her any-more. Hell — it's almost true.

*Matt moves to her and puts his arms around her. They kiss.*

**Matt:** Thanks.

**Violet:** No problem.

*The studio. David leans against the window staring at the canvas. There is a knock at the door.*

**David:** Yeah?

*Kryla enters.*

**Caption:** Calgary

**Kryla:** What I like about Calgary is it's metropolitan without being pretentious. Toronto's like a lady who's scared to get drunk because she might fall down. Calgary's like a lady who still knows how to get pissed and fall on her face once in a while.

**David:** Very good.

**Kryla:** Tomorrow's column. An Ode to Calgary.

**David:** Why don't you write something about how everyone in Calgary thinks they're far more attractive than they actually are?

**Kryla:** No point kicking a populace while it's down. *[Calgary's in a harsh recession]* Hard at work?

**David:** Fuck no.

**Kryla:** Stoned.

**David:** Completely. Toke?

**Kryla:** Makes my eyes bag. *[no]* Got anything to drink?

**David:** Antifreeze.

**Caption:** Numb

*Kryla moves to the fridge and gets straight vodkas as they speak.*

**David:** I have no life.

**Kryla:** You have plenty of life darling — and plenty of talent.

**David:** Everyone's waiting for that next show and I have nothing to paint.

**Kryla:** You need a lover.

**David:** Don't reduce it to that.

**Kryla:** Darling, you're just like me. You're happiest when you're being fucked regularly and in intense emotional pain. It's our nature. Don't fight it. Great art comes from the strangest places.

**David:** But I'm not making *[very loud]* ANY art.

**Kryla:** So go meet someone. You're rich now.

**Caption:** The Price

**David:** Ever since that show at AGO I've been hiding out. Someone's always sticking a microphone

in my face or phoning me for a quote. All that
controversy shit — and those TV shows. . . . Meet
someone? I can't even look people in the eye anymore. They all want something. I'm hiding.

**Kryla:** Paint moi.

**David:** You wouldn't pay me.

**Kryla:** No.

**David:** I did my best painting when I was a waiter.

**Kryla:** I did my best writing when I was a virgin. Life's
a barter system.

**Caption:** Spark

**David:** I need a job.

**Kryla:** As a what?

**David:** A waiter.

**Kryla:** You hated being a waiter.

**David:** You meet people. Overhear things. See new
faces.

**Kryla:** Shlep chow for dicks who don't tip.

**David:** It's real.

**Kryla:** What if someone recognizes you?

**David:** No one recognizes painters.

**Kryla:** You don't want people to think you've fallen on
hard times.

**David:** I'll go to some dive.

**Kryla:** It's beneath you.

**David:** I'm gonna do it. I am. Bragg Creek *[Calgary suburb]* or somewhere bizarre like that.

**Kryla:** Go ahead, David. Do it if you must, but take it from me these things never work. You have to find new inspirations — new children on meathooks and tattooed erect penises — to paint. But you have to find them in the world you live in now. Not the one you used to know. And it's not as easy to get a job as it used to be. You haven't had a job in ten years —

**David:** *Interjects.* Sometimes you are so Cruella. *[DeVille — a Disney villain]*

**Kryla:** It's the white streak in my hair and the cloud of yellow smoke that surrounds me.

**David:** I have to do this.

**Caption:** Meanwhile

*Matt is reading his ad to Violet.*

**Matt:** Wanted. Experienced waitperson for new restaurant. Part-time evenings only.

**Violet:** Brilliant. But I'd put responsible before experienced and bright before new.

**Matt:** Good idea. I figure if we can get someone to do three hours a night Wednesday to Saturday — the tips I make from the late tables and the other nights'll get us through.

**Violet:** You're a fuckin' genius.

**Matt:** How'd Trixie take it?

**Violet:** She'll live.

*Shannon enters.*

**Matt:** Hi.

**Shannon:** Yeah.

**Matt:** Table for one?

**Shannon:** Yeah.

**Matt:** Menu?

**Shannon:** Yeah.

**Matt:** You okay?

**Shannon:** Yeah.

**Matt:** Coffee?

**Shannon:** Yeah.

**Matt:** You sure you're okay?

**Shannon:** Coffee.

**Matt:** Yeah.

*Matt moves to the bar and gets coffee and a menu.*

**Shannon:** Just bring me whatever has the most calories.

**Matt:** Uh. . . . Shrimp in a cream sauce?

**Shannon:** Extra flour in the sauce.

**Matt:** You want a milkshake too?

**Shannon:** Vanilla.

**Caption:** The Want Ads

*David sits in the windowledge reading the paper.*

**David:** Experienced, responsible waitperson wanted for bright, new restaurant. Perfect.

*David circles the ad in the paper.*

*Shannon has finished eating. Matt is clearing the table.*

**Matt:** Anything else?

**Shannon:** I'm fine.

*Matt drops the bill on the table. Shannon sets money on the bill.*

**Matt:** Thanks for coming.

**Shannon:** Plezjh. *[pleasure]*

*Shannon stands to leave.*

**Matt:** 'night.

**Shannon:** Thanks.

*Shannon exits. Matt watches her through the window.*

**Violet:** Pretty attractive huh?

**Matt:** Was she?

**Violet:** Matt, quit lyin'.

**Matt:** She's nothing compared to you.

**Violet:** Fuckin' right.

**Caption:** Dead Dad

*The studio. Shannon is talking to David.*

**Shannon:** His fucking father died.

**David:** Great.

**Shannon:** He's gone back to Kalispell Montana for three weeks to bury him.

**David:** How Shane. *[the Alan Ladd movie]*

*David lights a joint. They share it.*

**David:** I'm going to get a job.

**Shannon:** A what?

**David:** As a waiter.

**Shannon:** Mildred Pierce. *[Joan Crawford got an Oscar]*

**David:** Smell that Oscar. Drink?

**Shannon:** Two. One glass.

**David:** Fridge.

*Shannon pours vodkas.*

**Shannon:** It's a good idea.

**David:** Really?

**Shannon:** You're so busy being David McMillan you don't know who you are anymore.

**David:** Jean Dixon, right! *[popular psychic]*

**Shannon:** My real mother.

**David:** Okay? *[are you?]*

**Shannon:** Who's got time to be depressed?

**Caption:** The Next Day

*David enters the restaurant. Matt is stocking the wine shelf.*

**David:** I'm here about the job.

**Matt:** Oh yeah.

**David:** I have a resume.

**Matt:** A resume?

**David:** It's been a while since I worked but you can see I have a great deal of experience.

**Matt:** It's only part-time.

**David:** I know.

**Matt:** It's not always that busy.

**David:** It's okay.

**Matt:** Tips aren't great.

**David:** Is there something wrong with the way I look?

**Matt:** No. No. Just — some of the applicants get pretty upset when you're not up-front with them from the beginning. It's just a few hours a night.

**David:** I need a job.

**Matt:** It's yours.

**David:** Just like that?

**Matt:** Hey, you had a resume.

**David:** Great.

**Caption:** Connect

*They shake hands.*

**Matt:** I'm Matt.

**David:** David.

**Matt:** Can you start tomorrow?

**David:** Sure. Black and whites?

**Matt:** Whatever. If you don't mind me saying so, you seem sorta . . . uh . . . *Searches for the right word.*

**Caption:** Old

**David:** Mature.

**Matt:** Yeah. Mature to want to work at a place like this.

**David:** *Shrugs.* I want a job.

*Violet enters with wet celery she stows in a jug of water under the bar as she speaks.*

**Violet:**  You're gonna have to run out for more of that cheap white wine we cook with.

**Matt:**  Dave. This is my wife. Violet. Dave's the new waiter.

**Violet:**  I'd shake your hand but I'm all wet, Dave.

**David:**  It's David, actually.

**Matt:**  Sorry.

**David:**  No problem.

**Violet:**  Short hours okay with you?

**David:**  They're fine.

**Violet:**  Good.

**David:**  Thanks. Nice to meet you both. See you tomorrow.

*David exits.*

**Violet:**  What a gentleman.

**Matt:**  Why do you say that?

**Violet:**  He didn't look at my tits when you introduced us.

**Matt:**  Really?

*The studio. David, Kryla, and Shannon hold drinks.*

**Kryla:**  Your job. *[A toast]*

**Shannon:**  Hear hear.

**Kryla:**  Stolen from some poor unfortunate who is much more in need of the money than you.

**David:**  I'll donate the money.

**Shannon:**  Lotta Hitchmanova. *[spokesperson for the Canadian branch of the Unitarian Service Committee for many years, heard on Canadian television throughout the 1960s and early 1970s]*

**David:**  Fifty-six Sparks Street Ottawa Four.

**Kryla:**  Freshen the antifreeze?

**David:**  No.

**Kryla:**  Pardon me?

**David:**  Work tomorrow.

**Kryla:**  Evening.

**David:**  Think I'll just blow a sploof and crash.

**Kryla:**  Guess it's off to the Ranchman's Club. I do so love to watch all of those broke oilmen crying into their scotch. Catch my column tomorrow.

**David:**  What's it about?

**Kryla:**  Lois Lane.

**Shannon:**  Oh I loved Lois Lane. She always wore the best hats and knew karate.

**Kryla:**  I'm doing a series on women of the 1960s. It's a little known fact and I don't share it with just anyone but Lois Lane is the reason I entered journalism.

**Shannon:** Really?

**David:** Pete Ross — Superboy's best friend — was a fag.

**Kryla:** No.

**David:** He knew that Superboy was Clark Kent and he didn't tell anyone. Not even Clark.

**Kryla:** That makes him a fag?

**David:** Yes. Catch up.

**Kryla:** Where exactly is this restaurant of yours anyway? I'd like to drop by.

**Caption:** No

**David:** I don't want anyone who knows me to know where it is.

**Kryla:** Oh really. . . .

**David:** I just want to be a waiter.

**Kryla:** *To Shannon. Paranoid.*

**Shannon:** Positively.

**David:** Just 'til I get settled in.

**Kryla:** Whatever. Love ya.

**David:** Mean it.

*Kryla exits.*

**Shannon:** You'll tell me where this restaurant is.

**David:** No.

**Shannon:** Evil.

**David:** 'night.

**Shannon:** Evil.

**Caption:** Their Bedroom

*Violet is taking out her contact lenses. Matt sits on the bed partially dressed. Reading the* **TV Guide.**

**Violet:** Mom's still bitchin' about dinner.

**Matt:** Tell her to come to the restaurant.

**Violet:** She didn't cook it she ain't eatin' it.

**Matt:** You explained to her how demanding it is to run a new restaurant?

**Violet:** Yeah.

**Matt:** Until it takes off we have no free time.

**Violet:** Mothers don't understand that shit. They just want you to do what they want you to do.

**Matt:** Right.

**Violet:** She's been kinda squirrely since Uncle Harv died.

**Matt:** Hey The Seventh Voyage of Sinbad is on.

**Violet:** Yeah?

**Matt:** Excellent Ray Harryhausen effects.

**Violet:** Wanna watch it and fuck during the commercials?

**Matt:** Sounds good.

**Violet:** I really like you.

**Caption:** Not About Dresses

*Shannon in bed. David opens Shannon's door and peeks in.*

**David:** Snatchbum.

**Shannon:** Fartface.

**David:** Still awake?

**Shannon:** C'min.

**David:** Thoughtful?

**Shannon:** Totally.

**David:** Scared.

**Shannon:** Nope.

**David:** Me.

**Shannon:** Why?

**David:** You think it's possible to change? Really change who we are — the things we do?

**Shannon:** I'm trying.

**David:** But you're changing the outer you to match the inner you. Think we can do it the other way round?

**Shannon:**   If we could I'da done it years ago.

**David:**   Is it right to even want to?

**Shannon:**   No harm in trying.

**Caption:**   The Future

*David sits on the bed next to Shannon and puts an arm around Shannon's shoulders.*

**David:**   Superman's engaged.

**Shannon:**   What?

**David:**   He proposed to Lois Lane as Clark Kent. Yesterday.

**Shannon:**   Jesus.

**David:**   I'm scared.

**Shannon:**   Don't worry. I'm here for you.

**Caption:**   Kal-El *[Superman's Kryptonian name]*

*Matt leans against the bar reading the newspaper. He talks to Violet through the pick-up opening to the kitchen.*

**Violet:**   He's an alien.

**Matt:**   Not.

**Violet:**   Krypton. He's a fuckin' alien. No Earth broad's gonna marry an alien.

*Violet enters from the kitchen carrying two five-litre containers of orange juice. Matt takes them out of her hands and stows them under the bar as they speak.*

**Matt:**   Spider-Man got married a coupla years ago.

**Violet:**   Spider-Man's from Earth.

**Matt:**   People from Earth can only marry other people from Earth?

**Violet:**   How does she even know if he's got a dick?

**Matt:**   He's got a dick.

**Violet:**   Mebbe his come's poison to humans.

**Matt:**   Superman's come is not poison.

*David enters.*

**David:**   Hi.

**Matt:**   Early too.

**David:**   I brought a billfold and a corkscrew.

**Violet:**   Restaurant's split half and half.

**David:**   Polish the silver?

**Violet:**   If ya want. Polish the fucking light fixtures if you want — just make sure you get the food to the table while it's hot and flip it as fast as you can.

**David:**   Gotcha.

**Violet:**   The place's simple, friendly and cheap.

**David:**   Simple, friendly and cheap.

**Violet:**   And fast.

**David:**   I give great fast.

**Violet:**   You better. Matt'll show you where everything is. I handle the kitchen. Don't fuck with my kitchen.

**David:**   Wouldn't dream of it.

**Matt:**   Come on. I'll show you where we keep the liquor.

**David:**   Great.

*David and Matt move to the stockroom as they speak. Violet exits to the kitchen.*

**Caption:**   The Stockroom

*Matt takes a package of cigarettes from behind a crate.*

**Matt:**   Vi's kinda outspoken.

**David:**   She's great.

**Matt:**   Let's smoke.

**David:**   Okay.

**Matt:**   I'm trying to quit. Have been for six months now. I don't like Violet to see me. Sure she knows — but we don't say anything as long as she doesn't see me.

**David:**   Ah.

**Matt:**   So whadaya think?

**David:**   Seems fine.

**Matt:**   A wedding present from Vi's mom. She wanted to make sure we had a future.

**David:** How long you been married?

**Matt:** Just over two years.

**David:** Kids?

**Matt:** Not yet. The restaurant.

**David:** Right.

**Matt:** Grab a dozen Blue [popular brand of Canadian beer] wouldja. We're gonna smell like smoke.

**David:** Blame it on me. I'm a smoker.

**Matt:** Good idea.

**Caption:** Men Smell

*A spot on Violet working in the kitchen.*

**Violet:** Different men smell different but all men smell different from woman. Men smell kind of like . . . vinegar and far away cat boxes . . . but nice too.

**Caption:** After The Rush

*David and Matt are clearing dishes.*

**David:** Short rush.

**Matt:** It gets a little better every day. You're real relaxed on the floor.

**David:** Guess it never goes away.

**Matt:** Your money okay?

**David:** Fine. You?

**Matt:** Oh yeah.

*Violet enters from the kitchen.*

**Violet:** Chan's gonna need help with the pots. It'll only take a few minutes.

**Matt:** Hon, you can't ask a waiter to help a dishwasher.

**Violet:** Trixie helped the dishwasher.

**Matt:** Trixie was simple.

**David:** That's all right.

**Matt:** You don't mind?

**David:** No.

**Matt:** Thanks man.

**David:** Plezjh.

*David exits to the kitchen.*

**Matt:** What's wrong?

**Violet:** Since when do waiters not help dishwashers?

**Matt:** Come on Vi. The guy's worked at some pretty good places. He's got a real way with customers — he shouldn't have to help Chan wash pots.

**Violet:** Are you going to start paying Chan for another hour every night then?

**Matt:** It's only six bucks.

**Violet:** Any comments on the food?

**Caption:**  Lie

**Matt:**  No.

*Violet puts her arms around Matt and kisses him. David enters. Violet and Matt break the kiss.*

**David:**  Chan's very quick.

**Violet:**  You restock the beer cooler??

**David:**  Hours ago. Incidentally, I had a couple comments about the food — the soup mostly. People said it was salty.

*David sits at a table and does his cash-out as they speak.*

**Violet:**  Oh?

**David:**  It's a sign the cook is developing a resistance to salt.

**Violet:**  Really?

**David:**  Someone else said their pork chops were dry.

**Violet:**  Dry.

**David:**  Of course, I got both these comments after the customers had paid and were on their way out or I would've notified you immediately. As it was I only had time to take their names and numbers. I thought you might want to contact them.

**Violet:**  What for?

**David:**  Well to . . . to deal with the problem of course. You don't want dissatisfied patrons discussing your restaurant with other people do you?

**Matt:** No.

**Violet:** Did anyone else say it was salty? I mean — one complaint doesn't —

**Matt:** *Cutting her off.* One of my tables said it too.

**Caption:** Run Away

**David:** I'd better go. Thanks. Had a great time.

*David exits.*

**Violet:** I gotta know about customer complaints, Matt. I gotta know so I can fix them.

**Matt:** But you always look so mad . . .

**Violet:** I'm not mad. I just look that way. I know how to cook. I hate it when I screw up.

**Matt:** I'll take care of it.

**Violet:** No. Gimme the phone number. I'll take care of it.

**Matt:** Sure?

**Violet:** They complained about the food — not the service.

**Caption:** I Need A Man

*Kryla enters. David is smoking a joint.*

**Kryla:** I have this irresistible need to have a man in my life.

**David:** Suppress it.

**Kryla:** Not that I'm going to fall in love of course. Not at my age. I've been around. The block. Four or five hundred times.

**David:** How old would he be?

**Kryla:** I'd prefer early twenties. You know. When their skin's still flawless and they've got a constant erection. But I'd accept thirtyish as well.

**David:** Fuck him immediately?

**Kryla:** Darling — one doesn't fuck anymore.

**David:** Forgot.

**Kryla:** I would let him feel me up in a car though.

**David:** Would you let him finger you?

**Kryla:** Laws, Darling — who wouldn't? More satisfying. Less yeast infections. Hey . . . you did that waitering thing tonight.

**David:** Yeah.

**Kryla:** And?

**David:** It was great.

**Kryla:** Oh. Good.

**David:** I'm gonna try and do some sketching.

**Kryla:** This is my cue to leave.

**David:** Love ya.

**Kryla:**   Mean it.

*Kryla exits. David picks up a pad of drawing paper and some charcoal.*

**Caption:**   Almost

*David stares at the blank paper for a long moment. He begins to sketch tentatively. Shannon enters.*

**Shannon:**   Randy.

**David:**   Randy?

**Shannon:**   Whatever happened to him?

**David:**   He left me to go back to his girlfriend.

**Shannon:**   Don't you just hate that?

**David:**   Men are such wonderful creatures.

**Shannon:**   Too bad they're all pricks.

**David:**   Really.

**Caption:**   Lovers

**Shannon:**   You should try living with someone some time.

**David:**   If the right person ever comes along.

**Shannon:**   It's nice.

**David:**   You still miss him?

**Shannon:**   Constantly. Completely.

**David:**   Shit.

**Shannon:**   Total Teresa Trance. *[I'm being overly sensitive and boring.]*

**David:**   No. It's okay. Really. We need to talk. Always. As much as you want.

**Shannon:**   I'd like to go to his grave.

**David:**   I'll make the martinis.

**Caption:**   Casual Conversations

*Matt and Violet in bed. Matt is picking his toenails. Violet reads a magazine.*

**Violet:**   Says in here most men fantasize about other people to keep their sex lives interesting.

**Matt:**   Yeah?

**Violet:**   You ever fantasize about other people?

**Caption:**   Yes

**Matt:**   No.

**Caption:**   Why

**Matt:**   Do you?

**Caption:**   No

**Violet:**   No.

**Caption:**   Thomas Dzus
                    1959 - 1988

*David and Shannon stand on Tom's grave. Each holds a martini glass filled with vodka.*

Michael J. Blankenship as David, Damian Baldet as Matt, and Shannon Rae
Lutz as Violet. *Photo: Sandy Underwood*

**Shannon:** We never really stood a chance.

**David:** How were we to know mindless ass fucking and intravenous drug use would lead to such heartbreak?

**Shannon:** I swallowed a fortune.

**David:** You sorry now?

**Shannon:** About what? Loving Tom? He was the best thing that ever happened to me — even if he was a bit too attached to the needle. Sucking scumbags off in the front seat of their cars? What else can someone like me do? It's not like they're gonna hire me at Fairweather or something.

**David:** You're beautiful.

**Shannon:** Will you promise to bury me in white taffeta?

**David:** I didn't know taffeta came in white.

**Shannon:** Comes in all flavours.

**David:** Would you like a tiara?

**Shannon:** Only if it's real diamonds. I can't abide zircons and I'm far too old for rhinestones.

**David:** Okay.

**Shannon:** It's kind of exciting.

**David:** Yeah?

**Shannon:** Who knows what happens. It could be the start of a whole new thing. Something beyond life.

Another adventure we don't know anything about yet.

**David:** I hope so.

**Shannon:** We think we know fucking everything. We think we've got it all figured out. But we don't know shit.

**Caption:** The Restaurant Day

*Matt is behind the bar mixing lime juice. Violet enters from the kitchen.*

**Violet:** You havta sign Wonder Boy's paycheck. I left it on your desk. And Chan's.

**Matt:** Right.

*The telephone rings. Violet grabs it.*

**Violet:** Monteray Diner. Yeah. Yeah. Yeah. Just a minute. *To Matt, without bothering to cover up the mouthpiece.* Mother. She's gonna slit her wrists if we cancel dinner again.

**Matt:** I don't remember committing to a dinner.

**Violet:** *Into telephone.* You listening?

**Matt:** We run a restaurant. We can't afford to go out for dinner.

**Violet:** *Into phone.* There ya have it.

**Matt:** When we're making some more money and things are running smoothly we'll be over for dinner.

**Violet:** *Into phone.* He's the boss. What? What? I'll ask. *To Matt.* How come you can't handle the place on your own for one night?

**Matt:** Because I've got to work the floor.

**Violet:** I thought that's why we got us a waiter.

**Matt:** Oh yeah.

**Violet:** *Into phone.* A light's breakin'.

**Matt:** I guess on a slow night . . .

**Violet:** *Into phone.* Monday.

**Matt:** Sure.

**Violet:** *Into phone.* I'll still have to work the dinner rush so don't expect me a second before eight. Great. Great. Great. Bye.

*Violet hangs up the phone.*

**Violet:** You sure you and Wonder Boy can handle the place?

**Matt:** Sure. It'll be fun to cook again.

**Violet:** I need a break anyway.

**Matt:** We could both use a break.

*David enters dressed for work.*

**David:** Fabulous weather. *[it's snowing]*

**Matt:** Hey.

**Violet:** Wonder Boy.

**David:** I'm hardly a boy.

**Violet:** Ah — yer all boys.

**David:** Any resos?

**Matt:** Two.

**Violet:** Everything's slow in February.

**Matt:** Smoking or non?

**David:** Why don't you take smoking and deal with the endless coffee refill people?

**Matt:** You always give me smoking and it's always the busiest side.

**Violet:** You guys need to refill salt and peppers tonight.

**David:** Did it yesterday.

**Violet:** *Starting to exit to kitchen.* Trust Wonder Boy.

**David:** It's true, Monkey Girl.

**Violet:** Don't call me Monkey Girl.

**David:** Don't call me Wonder Boy.

**Violet:** You wanna check the soup for me tonight?

**David:** Sure.

**Violet:** I've been laying off the salt.

**David:** You're still overcooking the pasta.

**Violet:** Yeah?

**David:** And I still say the radishes carved into roses as
. a garnish are too seventies.

**Violet:** What would you suggest?

**David:** Kale. You can get it in mauve now. It's very eye-
catching.

**Violet:** *Laughs.* Mauve kale. Jesus.

*Violet exits to the kitchen.*

**David:** What time's the first reso?

**Matt:** Seven-thirty.

**David:** Shit. *[it's only five]*

**Matt:** You know how to play crib?

**David:** No.

**Matt:** I'll teach you.

**David:** Okay.

**Caption:** Pricks

*Kryla and Shannon are in the studio looking through David's
sketchbooks.*

**Kryla:** What I truly want to know is why is it that the
penis is considered attractive and the vagina is
considered ugly? Why do we never discuss
scrotums?

**Shannon:** And how come in movies men always fuck with their pants on while the women are nude?

**Kryla:** It's a conspiracy. They know if we got to look at their shriveled genitalia as often as they get to look at ours we'd never take them seriously.

**Shannon:** Dicks are overrated. *Referring to sketch.* Isn't this you?

**Kryla:** Some years ago. I forgot all about it.

**Shannon:** You look like an axe-murderer.

**Kryla:** I was an axe-murderer. Thank God for Prozac.

*Matt and David are playing crib at the bar. Matt is counting David's hand.*

**Matt:** Fifteen two. Fifteen four. Fifteen six. Fifteen eight. A run is twelve and one for the Jack.

**David:** Genetically I'm not built for this.

**Matt:** It's not that hard.

**David:** You need publicity.

**Matt:** Do you know what it costs for an ad in the *Herald* or the *Sun*?

**David:** No.

**Matt:** Lots.

**David:** Look, why don't you sign me out now and take whatever else comes in?

**Matt:** It's only been an hour.

**David:**  Save yourself some money.

**Matt:**  Stay and have a beer.

**David:**  Sure.

*Matt gets two beers from behind the bar.*

**Matt:**  Man I gotta tell you you're great. You get these waiters with attitude, you know — not interested in the restaurant except when it's busy and they're pullin' in the tips and after that — bang — they're outa here. No clean up, no thank you — no nothing.

**David:**  Thanks.

**Matt:**  What else do you do? I mean you're not just a waiter right?

**Caption:**  Careful

**David:**  I . . . paint.

**Matt:**  Oh yeah.

**David:**  I've had a . . . few showings.

**Matt:**  I usta wanna draw comic books. I was really into it. Even drew a few full stories when I was in high school. I was pretty good.

**David:**  I used to collect comics.

**Matt:**  Me too.

**David:**  I'm a DC man myself.

**Matt:**  No way. DC sucks. Superman — Wonder Woman. Get real. Marvel's great.

**David:** Those are classic characters.

**Matt:** Boring.

**David:** Superman is not boring.

**Matt:** All right. Superman's a special case.

**David:** Superman transcends the medium.

**Matt:** Right.

*Violet enters from the kitchen, watching Matt and David.*

**Violet:** You guys got nothing to do?

**Matt:** Don't worry. I signed him out.

**Violet:** Great.

**David:** I was just about to leave actually.

**Matt:** Finish your beer.

**Violet:** What if someone came in and saw you guys sittin' around like this?

**Matt:** No one's come in yet.

**Violet:** This is pathetic.

**Matt:** Mebbe we should just shut it down for the night.

**David:** Bad idea. If someone should come by and find you not open when you're supposed to be open — well they're gonna be pissed off and they're gonna start talking and you just don't need that kinda PR.

**Violet:** What did we do without you?

**David:**  On the other hand — if it keeps snowing like this no one's gonna show.

**Violet:**  We'll give it another hour.

**Matt:**  You want another beer buddy?

**Caption:**  Buddy

**David:**  Buddy?

**Violet:**  What?

**David:**  Your husband just called me buddy.

**Violet:**  So?

**David:**  You guys know I'm gay . . . right?

**Caption:**  Gay

**Matt:**  Oh.

**Violet:**  Gay.

**David:**  It's not a big deal or anything . . . is it?

**Matt:**  No. [maybe]

**Violet:**  No. [yes]

**Caption:**  Queer

**Violet:**  You're a homosexual.

**David:**  Yeah.

**Violet:**  Wow.

**David:** I didn't mean for it to be a big thing. I assumed you knew. I mean I *am* a waiter.

**Violet:** You saying all waiters are fags?

**David:** No. Just lots of them.

**Matt:** Why's that?

**David:** I dunno. The crazy hours aren't a problem when you don't have a family we enjoy working with the public we do well in subservient positions. I dunno.

**Matt:** Lotsa fags are hairdressers too.

**Violet:** And guys who arrange flowers.

**David:** And guys who design dresses and people who make furniture and painters and writers and composers and — well — anything in the world that's pretty — we made it.

**Violet:** Like mauve kale.

**David:** We didn't make mauve kale — we just accessorized it.

**Matt:** Straight people make some nice stuff too.

**David:** Like what?

**Caption:** Television

**Violet:** Well . . .

**Caption:** Shopping Malls

**Violet:** Like . . . uh . . .

**Caption:** The Atom Bomb

**Matt:** Cowboy hats. Straight people made cowboy hats.

**Violet:** And Kentucky Fried Chicken.

**David:** Nope.

**Violet:** Colonel Sanders was a fag?

**David:** That's what I heard.

**Matt:** Get out!

**David:** I'm joking. Relax. I'm gonna run before we're all snowed in. See you tomorrow.

**Violet:** 'night.

**Matt:** Tomorrow.

**David:** Count on it.

*David exits.*

**Caption:** Alien Among Us

**Violet:** Well.

**Matt:** Jeez.

**Violet:** I never woulda known.

**Matt:** The guy who built the Empire State Building was straight.

**Violet:** We can't afford many more nights like this, Matt.

**Caption:**   Not The Buddy Thing

*David is in the studio with Shannon.*

**David:**   The husband's interesting . . . he's one of those
men . . . you know those men who look at you like
they want to . . .

**Shannon:**   *Interjects.* Fuck you?

**David:**   Share a secret.

**Shannon:**   Dangerous.

**David:**   I think I make his wife nervous.

**Shannon:**   Beware the nervous wife.

**David:**   They know men too well.

**Shannon:**   So you've got a buddy.

**David:**   I find the shape of his skull fascinating.

**Shannon:**   Nice?

**David:**   Squiz. *[exquisite]*

**Caption:**   Advice

*Kryla enters carrying a martini glass half-filled with straight
vodka. She delivers this speech with great rapidity.*

**Kryla:**   So, simply put, the dilemma is this. Say you
knew someone quite well and you liked them quite
a lot and they seemed to like you quite a lot too —
with me?

**David:**   Yeah.

**Kryla:**  And say you had never seen this person — you got to know each other with letters the telephone whatever and now this person wanted to meet you and you really wanted to meet them but say you'd told maybe one or two tiny untruths during those letters or phone calls or whatever — and now you're afraid to meet this person that you know but have never seen because you're not everything you said you were. What would you do?

**Shannon:**  Is this one of those phone line things?

**Kryla:**  Of course not. It. . . . Well yes it is — it is exactly one of those phone line things.

**David:**  What did you tell him?

**Kryla:**  That I was twenty-six.

**Shannon:**  What?!

**Kryla:**  I don't know what came over me. As soon as I heard his voice I was possessed by every female babysitter I'd had as a child and lied my fool head off. He sounded just like my favorite Uncle Phil.

**Shannon:**  Uncle Phil damage.

**David:**  Twenty-six?

**Kryla:**  I meant to say thirty.

**Shannon:**  Good luck.

**Kryla:**  In the right light. If I've had lots of sleep.

**Shannon:**  And they've had lots of heroin.

**Kryla:** Shannon, please. . . .

**David:** Well what do you want to do?

**Kryla:** Stun him and stick him in a freezer until I've had cosmetic surgery.

**David:** Call him and tell him the truth.

**Kryla:** I can't.

*Kryla goes to the fridge and pours herself another vodka.*

**Kryla:** Oh I hate my mother. I just hate her. Why weren't we warned?

**Shannon:** Too busy ironing.

**Caption:** Dykes Are Lucky

**Kryla:** Dykes are lucky. They're the only people who meet lovers who care about them as people. I wish I was a dyke. Only thinking about it makes me sick. The Eaton's catalogue did this to me. Ginger on Gilligan's Island did this to me.

**David:** Tell him the truth.

**Kryla:** I hate it when you sound like my father.

**David:** Have to do it.

**Kryla:** I know.

**Caption:** Pry

**Kryla:** How's the tip money?

**David:** Fine.

**Kryla:** Having fun?

**David:** Yep.

**Kryla:** Don't you trust me?

**David:** It's not about trust. I really need some place where my life doesn't intrude.

**Kryla:** Just let me come and check it out. I'll pretend not to know you. I'll write something nice about it in the column.

**David:** No.

**Kryla:** It's driving me mad. You know that.

**David:** Mad becomes you.

**Caption:** Fathers

*Matt is setting tables. David joins him.*

**Matt:** My father left when I was eleven years old. I was the youngest so I don't remember him very well. My sisters do. Teaspoon.

*David hands Matt a teaspoon.*

**David:** Sometimes I feel like the only men who stayed with their families in the seventies were the ones fucking their kids.

**Matt:** Nice.

**David:** Gotta knife?

*Matt hands David a knife.*

**Matt:** What about your dad?

**David:** My old man made Fred Flintstone look like Oscar Wilde.

**Matt:** Didn't get along?

**David:** Beat me.

**Matt:** Oh.

**David:** Drunk too.

**Matt:** I wanna see your paintings sometime.

**Caption:** Retreat

**Matt:** Vi's gonna be at her mom's late. I thought we could get a case of beer and maybe go over to your place after we close up.

**David:** I have a roommate.

**Matt:** Is this roommate like a roommate roommate or a roommate?

**David:** We're not lovers.

**Matt:** Into it?

**David:** I'm actually quite tired.

**Matt:** Sure.

**David:** Another night.

**Matt:** Yeah.

**David:** I do have time for a joint.

**Matt:**   Excellent.

**David:**   Got a match?

*Matt hands David a number of books of matches from behind the bar.*

**Matt:**   Take a handful. Pass 'em around.

*David stuffs a number of the matchbooks in his pocket.*

**David:**   Mercy. *[merci]*

*David lights a joint. They share it.*

**Matt:**   Wanna go to my place instead? I have Nintendo.

**David:**   Some other night.

**Matt:**   You don't like straight people, do you?

**David:**   Some of my best friends are straight.

**Matt:**   Really?

**David:**   Only the women.

**Matt:**   We're not all the same.

**David:**   No?

**Caption:**   No

*Kryla is with Shannon in the studio. They're drinking. Kryla is very agitated.*

**Kryla:**   Of course he didn't show. I knew he wouldn't.
I only waited twenty minutes.

**Shannon:**   Obviously he misrepresented himself, too.

**Kryla:**   The telephone's no way to meet a lover.

**Shannon:**   Well bars don't work either.

**Kryla:**   Blind dates are a horror show.

**Shannon:**   What else is there?

**Kryla:**   Canada Post.

*Their bedroom. Matt sits on the bed playing Nintendo. Violet enters.*

**Violet:**   Things okay at the place?

**Matt:**   Yeah.

**Violet:**   Busy?

**Matt:**   No.

**Violet:**   No?

**Matt:**   No.

**Violet:**   What's on your mind?

**Matt:**   Can't get past Magneto. *[he's playing X-Men.]*

**Violet:**   That's not what I meant.

**Matt:**   Nothing.

**Violet:**   Could you turn the Nintendo off?

*Matt turns the Nintendo off.*

**Violet:**   I know when something's bothering you.

**Matt:**  I don't really have any friends here.

**Violet:**  What about me?

**Matt:**  I mean except you.

*She snuggles up to him.*

**Violet:**  Aren't I enough?

**Matt:**  Sure.

**Caption:**  The Haunting

*David is sleeping in his bed. Shannon enters his room and sits on the edge of the bed. David wakes.*

**Shannon:**  Ghost in my room.

**David:**  What?

**Shannon:**  Tom.

**David:**  What?

**Shannon:**  He keeps walking around — like he's looking for a place to lie down but can't find one.

**David:**  What?

**Shannon:**  My dead lover's ghost is in my room and I can't get to sleep.

*David gets out of bed.*

**David:**  Oh. I'll take care of it.

**Shannon:**  Don't be mean.

**David:**   Firm.

**Shannon:**   Perf. *[perfect]*

*David exits.*

**Caption:**   When He Fucks Me

*A spotlight on Matt and Violet. He is fucking her.*

**Caption:**   Something Held Back

*Violet moans in pleasure. Matt's breathing is heavy and ragged.*

**Caption:**   Exorcise

*David enters Shannon's room.*

**David:**   Tom . . . you've got to leave Shannon alone. He's not ready to see you yet. Tom . . . you're not wanted here.

*There is the sound of a sad moan. It gradually fades. Shannon enters.*

**Shannon:**   Did you see him?

**David:**   No.

**Shannon:**   He was here.

**David:**   I believe you.

**Shannon:**   Do you ever think that like there's a whole lotta shit in the world we don't know how to see yet?

**David:**   Yes.

**Caption:** No Release

*Matt and Violet are still fucking. He suddenly withdraws and rolls off her.*

**Matt:** I can't come.

**Violet:** I hate it when you can't come. *[feels she's failed]*

**Matt:** It's not your fault.

**Violet:** Your dick sure gets small fast.

**Matt:** Shuddup.

**Violet:** It's cute.

**Matt:** Cute?!

**Violet:** I meant awesome.

**Matt:** That's what I thought.

**Caption:** Late

*The studio. David is pulling his jacket on. Shannon watches him.*

**Shannon:** Where are you off to?

**David:** Trax, for the stripper.

**Shannon:** Can't abide that place. Reminds me of a mobile home.

**David:** Gotta get sucked off.

*Shannon notices David's open sketchbook.*

**Shannon:**   You've been working.

**David:**   Just rough stuff.

**Shannon:**   What . . . is this exactly?

**David:**   Matt's forehead.

**Shannon:**   Ah. When are you planning to get around to the rest of him?

**David:**   I don't know.

*Their bedroom. Violet sits looking out the window. Matt watches her from the bed.*

**Violet:**   Wonder Boy's fag thing ever bother you?

**Matt:**   He's a good waiter.

**Violet:**   I think Uncle Harv was a fag when he was young. He never got married.

**Matt:**   Your Uncle Harv wasn't a fag; he was a bachelor.

**Violet:**   What do two men do together?

**Matt:**   Whatever they do with women. Only less holes I guess.

**Violet:**   Do you think they kiss each other?

**Matt:**   I don't know.

**Violet:**   Kinda gross huh?

**Matt:**   Kinda.

**Caption:**   Self-Esteem Strikeout

*A spot on David walking down the street alone.*

**David:**   Fat. Ugly. Old. Boring. That's why no one ever hits on you. That's why no one ever takes you home. Fat. Ugly. Old. Boring.

*Shannon is in the studio watching an infomercial on the television. Kryla enters, quite drunk.*

**Kryla:**   Where's David?

**Shannon:**   Trax.

**Kryla:**   That place horrifies me. Why are you up so late?

**Shannon:**   Tom's ghost woke me up.

**Kryla:**   Oh. Anyway, I was at this wine and cheese at the Centre *[For the Performing Arts]* that was too whiney and too cheezy and it suddenly dawned on me I'm not married.

**Shannon:**   Really?

**Kryla:**   I'm thirty-eight years old and I'm not married. How did this happen?!

*A light rises on David who is on the telephone.*

**Caption:**   A Month

**David:**   No. Sorry. I'm not giving any interviews right now. Not even to the CBC. Sorry. When I have another showing. Thanks.

*David hangs up the phone as Shannon enters.*

**Shannon:**   And just when are you planning to have another showing?

**David:**   I've been doing a lot of preliminaries actually.

**Shannon:**   Has the job helped?

**David:**   I think so. I feel . . . stimulated again.

**Shannon:**   Good.

**David:**   Why are you all dolled up?

**Shannon:**   *Like a really bad kids' show host.* It's Psychological Evaluation Time!

**David:**   Already?

**Shannon:**   Dr. Hoocheewatsit ran out of bereavement leave.

**David:**   *Not enthusiastic.* Great.

**Shannon:**   David, I know you don't approve but I don't care what you think. This is for me. Me me me me me. Now kiss me and wish me good luck because I'm special and I deserve this.

*David kisses Shannon.*

**David:**   Good luck.

**Shannon:**   We could celebrate . . . if you're not working tonight.

**David:**   I should be off early. It's been dead.

**Shannon:**   I'll chill the champagne.

**David:**   I'll rent The Christine Jorgenson Story. *[first sex change]*

*Kryla enters carrying an armful of envelopes.*

**Kryla:**   Seventeen replies.

**Shannon:**   Gotta run.

**Kryla:**   Is it me?

**Shannon:**   Vaginal appointment.

**Kryla:**   Mean ya.

**Shannon:**   Love it.

*Shannon exits. David lights a joint as he and Kryla speak. He uses a pack of the restaurant matches from his pocket, laying them on the table when he is done.*

**Kryla:**   So I put an ad in the personals section of the *Herald* and I got seventeen replies.

**David:**   Why are you doing this?

**Kryla:**   Because I can. Because I must. Because I am a writer. Also, you never know who you're going to meet if you don't try.

*Kryla notices the matches.*

**David:**   And?

**Kryla:**   The ad was simple. Attractive, successful woman . . . fortyish . . . well established and adventurous — I was careful not to misrepresent myself — seeks attractive man over thirty for companionship. Well laws, darling, I got tonsa letters from all these hideous men who fancy themselves to be attractive.

**David:**   Gonna reply to any of them?

**Kryla:**   Not this herd. Incidentally Paula at the CBC called me for your number. She wants to —

**David:**   I've got nothing to talk to Paula about.

**Kryla:**   Talk about being a waiter.

**David:**   You didn't tell her . . .

**Kryla:**   *Cutting him off.* Of course not.

**David:**   Good.

**Caption:**   Take Them

*Kryla slips the matches into her pocket.*

**Kryla:**   Let's go to a bar.

**David:**   I'm working tonight.

**Kryla:**   Really. Too bad.

**Caption:**   Goodbye David

*The restaurant. Matt is polishing glasses. Violet is slicing limes.*

**Violet:**   We can't afford a second waiter. Just can't.

**Matt:**   Shit.

**Violet:**   I like him too.

**Matt:**   He's the best waiter we've had.

**Violet:**   Mebbe — when things pick up — you can hire him back. We've got to do it, Matt.

**Matt:**   Yeah yeah.

*Shannon enters, taking a table.*

**Matt:**   Hi.

**Shannon:**   Coffee.

**Matt:**   You got it.

*Violet exits to the kitchen.*

**Shannon:**   *Depressed.* This smoking?

**Matt:**   Sure.

**Shannon:**   Would you find me a cigarette?

**Matt:**   I'll have to go to the back for it.

**Shannon:**   Please do.

*Matt exits. Shannon sips her coffee. David enters dressed for work. He and Shannon see each other immediately.*

**Caption:**   What

*David glances around quickly, then moves to Shannon furiously.*

**David:**   What the hell are you doing here?

**Shannon:**   Having coffee. My doctor's right across the street.

**David:** Shit.

**Shannon:** This is where you work?

**David:** Don't let on that you know me.

**Shannon:** Right.

*Matt enters with a cigarette for Shannon. It is on a saucer and has a package of matches with it.*

**Matt:** Hey, man.

**David:** Hi, Matt.

*Shannon puts the cigarette in her mouth. Matt lights it for her.*

**Shannon:** How much for the coffee?

**Matt:** Don't worry about it.

**Shannon:** Thank you.

**Matt:** You're not done.

**Shannon:** I know, but I just . . . well I just have to go.
Thanks for the coffee . . . and the smoke.

**Matt:** My pleasure.

*Shannon exits.*

**Matt:** She is one majestic babe.

**David:** Positively Mount Rushmorian. Resos?

**Matt:** No. This recession's endless.

**David:** This isn't a recession. It's the way things are
now.

**Matt:** We've gotta talk . . . .

**David:** I don't like the sound of that.

*Kryla enters.*

**Kryla:** Can I get a coffee?

*David and Matt turn to her.*

**Caption:** Shit

**Matt:** Sure.

**Kryla:** Thank you. So much.

**Matt:** I'll take it.

**David:** Right.

**Matt:** What? *[what's wrong?]*

**David:** Nothing.

**Caption:** How

*Matt moves behind the bar for coffee. Kryla addresses David.*

**Kryla:** Excuse me?

**David:** Yes?

**Kryla:** Have you got a match?

**David:** Yes.

**Kryla:** Oh silly me. I do have matches.

*Kryla produces the matches and hands them to David. Matt approaches with coffee.*

Ian Gelder as David
and Jude Akuwudike
as Shannon
*Photo: Sean Hudson*

Kent Staines as David and Christopher Peterson as Shannon.
*Photo: Kristina Hahn*

**David:**  Silly you.

**Matt:**  If it's stale I'll make fresh.

**Kryla:**  What do you have for dessert?

**Matt:**  Uh . . . *[he doesn't know]*

**David:**  Carrot cake, cherry cheesecake, vanilla ice cream . . .

**Kryla:**  I'll try the carrot cake.

**Matt:**  Coming right up.

*Violet enters from the kitchen. She sees Kryla and starts to head back into the kitchen.*

**Violet:**  Dinner?

**Matt:**  *Shakes his head.* Why don't you head home.

**Violet:**  Sure?

**Matt:**  Sure.

*Violet kisses Matt quickly as he cuts the carrot cake.*

**Violet:**  See you there.

*Violet exits.*

**Violet:**  'night Wonder Boy.

**David:**  'night Monkey Girl.

**Kryla:**  Wonder Boy?

*Matt serves the cake to Kryla.*

**Matt:**  She likes to kid him.

**Kryla:**  He seems most kiddable.

**Matt:**  You look familiar.

**Kryla:**  I have a newspaper column.

**Matt:**  The *Sun*. Right.

**Kryla:**  The *Herald*. Wrong.

**Matt:**  Right.

**Kryla:**  This cake is very good.

**Matt:**  My wife bakes it herself.

**Kryla:**  How rural. It's fabulous. What a charming room.
I'm so glad I dropped by.

**Matt:**  Where did you hear about us?

**Kryla:**  Actually a friend recommended you.

**Matt:**  Who?

**Kryla:**  This artist friend of mine.

**David:**  More coffee? It's very hot.

**Kryla:**  I really should be going.

**Matt:**  You hardly touched your cake.

**Kryla:**  It was wonderful. *Takes money from her purse and
hands it to Matt.* Really. I have a slight eating disor-
der. Lovely restaurant. What is your name? I'd like
to mention you in my column tomorrow.

**Matt:** Matt Engles.

**Kryla:** And it's *looks at the matchbook* the Monteray Diner, right?

**Matt:** Yes.

**Kryla:** Thank you so much. Good night.

*Kryla exits. Matt watches her through the window.*

**Matt:** Women.

**David:** What did you want to talk to me about?

**Matt:** I love workin' with you man.

**David:** You've got to fire me.

**Matt:** Just lay you off until things pick up.

**David:** I'll work for tips.

**Matt:** I can't afford to split them.

**David:** You can have them. I just want to work.

**Matt:** Mebbe in the spring . . . .

**David:** Business is gonna pick up. That woman who just came in. She's gonna write about you.

**Matt:** One blurb.

**David:** It won't be one blurb. She'll mention you a lot over the next few weeks. I know she will.

**Matt:** How?

**David:** I have a feeling for these things.

**Matt:** David, I can't. . . .

**David:** Don't let me go. Give me another week. It'll pick up.

**Matt:** I almost believe you.

**David:** Just watch.

*A light on Violet in their bedroom.*

**Violet:** You didn't lay him off?

*Matt joins Violet.*

**Matt:** He offered to work for free. What could I say to that?

**Violet:** Say "you're fired." People don't work for free. It's weird.

**Matt:** That woman that was there when you left writes for the *Sun*. She's gonna mention us in her column tomorrow.

**Violet:** Get out.

**Matt:** Took my name and everything.

**Violet:** Could help.

**Matt:** Don't want to turn around and have to hire another waiter.

**Violet:** One week.

**Caption:** Something Else

**Matt:** We spend an awful lot of time together.

**Violet:** We're married. That's how it works.

**Caption:** Kryla's Place

*Kryla and David are there.*

**David:** I want you to write about it.

**Kryla:** I'd planned to mention it . . .

**David:** No. I want you to rave about it. I want you to drop the name in your column at least twice this week.

**Kryla:** Why would I possibly do that?

**David:** Because they're going to go under if they don't get some asses in those chairs.

**Kryla:** It's a tough world.

**David:** And because you owe me.

**Kryla:** That place gets hot and someone's gonna recognize you sooner or later.

**David:** I'll deal with it.

**Kryla:** I bet those plebes don't even know who you really are.

**David:** And it's gonna stay that way.

**Kryla:** Not forever, darling. Antifreeze?

**David:** Small one.

*Kryla gets drinks as they speak.*

**Kryla:** She's married to that boy . . .

**David:** He's at least twenty . . .

**Kryla:** Two —

**David:** *Very defensive.* Eight —

**Kryla:** You've got a crush on him.

**David:** I do not!

**Kryla:** Uh huh.

**David:** So you'll do it?

**Kryla:** You're sure that's what you want?

**David:** Yes.

**Kryla:** I suppose — ethically — I should go back and try the food. Was the carrot cake a fair indication?

**David:** Yeah. She's a good cook and improving all the time.

**Kryla:** Anything else I should include?

**David:** Say it's fun.

**Kryla:** Gotcha.

*The studio. Shannon sits in the chair in front of the blank canvas. David enters, grabs his dope box and begins to roll a joint.*

**Shannon:**   They said no.

**David:**   Your health is too fragile.

**Shannon:**   I'm dying anyway.

**David:**   We're all dying.

**Shannon:**   Yeah. But I get to plan for my death.

**David:**   You win the sympathy vote.

**Shannon:**   You never wanted me to have this operation.

**David:**   No.

**Shannon:**   It's important to me.

**David:**   Why? You are who you are whether or not you've got a vagina.

**Shannon:**   Why is everyone so scared to let people change?

**David:**   I love you no matter who you are.

**Shannon:**   I'm a woman.

**David:**   Are you? I've never thought of you that way. You've always been something else — in between. And you're always changing your mind. You are. You used to get so close to doing it then back off.

**Shannon:**   Difficult decision.

**David:**   Maybe this is exactly what you're meant to be.

**Shannon:**   A freak.

**David:** We're all a fuckin' sideshow. Don't waste energy on shit you can't control.

**Shannon:** Tom came earlier. I talked to him for a while. I'm okay depressed okay depressed okay.

**David:** Anything I can do?

**Shannon:** Light that joint.

**David:** How much longer 'til our generation legalizes dope?

**Shannon:** *Glances at watch.* Twenty minutes.

**Caption:** Prepare

**David:** I have seen the face of horror and it is Betty Rubble. *[I've got some bad news]*

**Shannon:** Oh Jesus. Who'd we lose?

**David:** Trent.

**Shannon:** Trent was a brilliant dancer.

**David:** Great abs.

**Shannon:** He wasn't alone?

**David:** Mac says he was in a hospice in Vancouver.

**Shannon:** Good.

**David:** I'm not sure, but I don't think this is how it's supposed to work.

**Shannon:** What?

**David:** Death. Life. Whatever we're calling it these days. I mean, our grandparents are supposed to be experiencing this. Not us.

**Shannon:** Now we know why old people always look so sad.

**David:** Fags and senior citizens.

**Shannon:** *Buzzer noise.* Who are people who've seen too much, Alex. [*as in* Jeopardy!]

**David:** Correct.

**Caption:** Babies

*Matt and Violet are at the restaurant cleaning in the kitchen.*

**Violet:** I'll be thirty in four months.

**Matt:** Not yet.

**Violet:** What's this problem you've got with children?

**Matt:** Vi, I told you right after we started going out I'm not really into kids.

**Violet:** Never?

**Caption:** Never

**Matt:** When the restaurant gets off the ground we'll talk about it. We can't afford them until then anyway.

**Violet:** Right.

*Violet picks up a very large box of frozen food to move it.*

**Matt:**   Let me get that.

**Violet:**   I can handle it.

**Matt:**   It's heavy.

**Violet:**   I'm strong.

**Matt:**   I thought — if you didn't mind — I'd go out for a beer or something after work tonight.

**Caption:**   No

**Violet:**   You don't hafta ask my permission for that stuff, Matt.

**Matt:**   I thought I'd call Manny.

**Violet:**   Manny's a fuckin' slut.

**Matt:**   I haven't seen him for a long time.

**Violet:**   You go out with Manny and you'll have women sniffin' around you all night. Go out with someone else.

**Matt:**   Like who?

*David enters with a* Herald.

**David:**   See the paper today?

**Matt:**   Told you it'd run.

**Violet:**   He had us watching the *Sun*.

**David:**   You want a hand with that box?

*Matt takes the paper from David and reads it greedily. Violet is attempting to move the box to a higher shelf.*

**Violet:**  No.

**Matt:**  *Reading.* She's strong.

**David:**  Whatever.

**Matt:**  Listen.

**Caption:**  The Review

**Matt:**  *Reading aloud.* Although it's a homey and simple eatery the Monteray Diner is one of the city's best kept secrets. The proprietor, one Matt English . . .

**Violet:**  Engles!

**David:**  Get used to it.

**Matt:**  . . . and his wife serve up the kind of uncompli- cated fare that causes the customer to recollect those delicious, hearty meals served by a favourite aunt.

**Violet:**  She called me a fuckin' aunt!

*Violet drops the box.*

**Matt:**  This is gonna be very good for business.

**David:**  Now if you were smart you'd capitalize on this with some kind of discount advertised in one of the papers.

**Matt:**  Y'gotta spend some money to make some — right?

**David:** Right.

**Violet:** We don't have any money.

**David:** You will.

**Violet:** Sure that?

**David:** Yes.

**Matt:** He knows everything.

**David:** Almost everything.

*David casually sets the box on the shelf Violet was trying to reach.*

**Violet:** He know how to keep you out of trouble?

**David:** What?

**Matt:** Sure he does.

**David:** What?

**Violet:** The husband needs a night on his own. Wanna keep an eye on him for me?

**David:** I charge extra for babysitting.

**Violet:** I'm good for it.

**David:** Okay.

**Matt:** Great.

**Caption:** The Dead

*Shannon alone.*

**Shannon:** I have this dream about my friend Murray who died in 1987 and I run into him in the shaving cream lane of the drug store and I'm like shocked because she's supposed to be dead and he laughs and says it's fabulous, nothing like you think and he's just about to tell me how to be alive again and I wake up.

**Caption:** Closed

*The restaurant. David is about to light a joint.*

**Matt:** Seemed like we were gonna get juiced for a minute there.

**David:** People read the paper.

**Matt:** Guess so.

**David:** Take an ad.

**Matt:** All right. Whadaya wanna do?

**David:** Doesn't matter. Little puff first?

**Matt:** Can we wait til Vi leaves?

**David:** Mebbe she'd like to share it.

**Matt:** No.

*Violet enters dressed to leave. David palms the joint.*

**Violet:** You gonna be late?

**Matt:** Not too.

**Violet:** Call.

**Matt:**   Sure.

*Matt and Violet kiss.*

**Violet:**   *To David.* Keep him outa the gutter.

**David:**   Do my best.

*Violet exits.*

**Caption:**   The Street

*Matt and David walk down the street as David lights the joint.*

**Matt:**   We should go to Republic. *[alternative bar catering to a younger, ambiguous crowd]*

**David:**   *Lighting joint.* Neither of us is wearing enough black.

**Matt:**   We could change.

**David:**   What kinda world do we live in when black clothing and black lights are in at the same time?

*They share the joint.*

**Matt:**   Sometimes the music's okay.

**David:**   Electric Avenue?

**Matt:**   Meat markets. Someplace we can talk.

**David:**   King Eddy?

**Matt:**   Perf. Great doobage. *[pot]*

**David:**   Let's walk.

**Matt:** Excellent.

**David:** Warmed up.

**Matt:** Chinook. *[warm winter wind]*

**Matt:** Why don't you have some guy in your life?

*David and Matt are now in a bar. They sit at a table and drink beer.*

**Caption:** I'm Ugly

**David:** I dunno.

**Matt:** I think lotsa guys want your big dick.

**David:** It's what every man in this room is thinking about right now.

**Matt:** Don't take this the wrong way or anything . . .

**David:** What?

**Matt:** You don't seem . . .

**David:** What?

**Caption:** Normal

**Matt:** Faggy.

**David:** What's faggy?

**Matt:** Femmy.

**David:** Neither do you.

**Matt:** Do I seem like I'm straight?

**David:**   Intermittently.

**Matt:**   Great night at the restaurant.

**David:**   Yeah.

**Matt:**   Hope it keeps up.

**David:**   It will.

**Matt:**   How do you know?

**David:**   I have a feeling for these things.

**Matt:**   Yeah?

**David:**   You're going to be mentioned in the paper again.

**Matt:**   You sure?

**David:**   Positive.

**Matt:**   Who are you?

**David:**   Superman.

**Caption:**   Impulse

*Matt puts one hand on the side of David's face, touching it gently. They stare at one another.*

**Caption:**   Heat

**David:**   Mebbe you should go.

**Matt:**   Yeah.

*Matt takes his hand from David's face. He leaves.*

**Caption:** Yes

*Shannon in the studio.*

**Shannon:** I smell acrylic and gesso.

*David moves into the studio and begins mixing paint.*

**David:** Yep.

**Shannon:** What's happened?

**David:** My muse finally gave me a boner.

**Shannon:** You actually gonna paint?

**David:** You betcha.

**Shannon:** You'll be up all night.

**David:** *Thrilled.* Uh huh.

**Shannon:** Good luck.

**David:** 'night.

*Shannon exits. David finishes mixing the paint and sits, lighting a joint. He stares at the canvas.*

**Caption:** Ideas

**David:** Men.

**Caption:** Bliss

*David paints a single stroke onto the canvas.*

**David:** Oh yeah.

*David paints another stroke.*

**David:**   Yeah.

**Caption:**   Flight

*David's painting becomes smoother, less choppy. Matt speaks without ever entering the light.*

**Matt:**   I always had a best friend.

**David:**   Through the head into your hand.

**Matt:**   Someone like me.

**David:**   Paint.

**Matt:**   Me.

**David:**   Matt.

**Caption:**   Matt

*Matt and Violet's bedroom. Violet yells at Matt who's in the bathroom.*

**Violet:**   Matt!

**Matt:**   *Off.* What?

**Violet:**   Didja have a good time?

**Matt:**   *Off.* Yeah.

**Violet:**   Whaja do?

**Matt:**   *Off.* Nothing.

**Violet:**   Nothing?

**Matt:** *Off.* Had a few beers.

**Violet:** That it?

**Matt:** *Off.* That's it.

**Violet:** What're you doing in there?

**Matt:** *Off.* Nothing.

**Violet:** Nothing?

**Matt:** *Off.* Taking a dump!

**Violet:** Oh.

*Shannon's bedroom. Shannon lies on the bed. Kryla is showing Shannon the replies to her ad.*

**Kryla:** A guy with a hook, a guy who really isn't inter-ested in a relationship — but would be interested in having me save my farts in plastic bags for him — and a Christian gentleman from Airdrie. *[small town outside of Calgary]*

**Shannon:** Try the Christian.

**Kryla:** I'd rather date Ted Bundy.

**Shannon:** Less misogynistic.

**Kryla:** Is David interested in someone?

**Shannon:** No. Why?

**Kryla:** He's acting like he's interested in someone.

**Shannon:** How's that?

**Kryla:**   He gets very distant and distracted. Hard to reach. I've never liked it.

**Shannon:**   He's been painting.

**Kryla:**   Really?

*The restaurant. David and Matt are resetting the tables together. They do this with great efficiency and ease as they speak.*

**David:**   I've got something I want to show you.

**Matt:**   What?

**David:**   Have to show you.

**Matt:**   Where?

**David:**   My place.

**Matt:**   Tonight?

**David:**   If you can.

**Matt:**   Let me handle it.

*Violet enters with her jacket.*

**Violet:**   Almost done?

**Matt:**   Actually we've got to rotate everything in the beer coolers.

**Violet:**   I thought you did that last week?

**Matt:**   Never got to it.

**Violet:**   Shit honey . . . I'm exhausted.

**Matt:**   Why don't you go ahead. I'll meet you at home.

**Violet:**   Don't be too late.

**Matt:**   Promise.

**Violet:**   G'night boys.

**David:**   'night, Vi.

*Violet exits. David and Matt finish setting up.*

**David:**   We really going to rotate the coolers?

**Matt:**   Did it last week.

**David:**   Lying prick.

*Matt laughs.*

**Caption:**   The Studio

*David and Matt move into the studio area. The canvas is covered with a sheet. David is pouring drinks.*

**Matt:**   *Impressed.* I walk by this building all the time. I had no idea it looked like this from the outside.

**David:**   Renovated it myself.

**Matt:**   These antiques?

**David:**   Some of them. That's actually a very expensive reproduction.

**Matt:**   Your family got money or something like that?

**David:**   Something like that.

*Shannon enters.*

**Shannon:**   Sorry.

**David:**   My pig daughter Scrunta.

**Matt:**   You came into the restaurant.

**Shannon:**   That's right.

**Matt:**   I'm Matt.

*They shake.*

**Shannon:**   Shannon.

**Matt:**   I didn't know you knew each other.

**Shannon:**   David's been kind enough to give me the loft
    in the back.

**Matt:**   There's more to this place?

**David:**   This is just my studio.

**Matt:**   You have a bed in your studio?

**Shannon:**   He lives in his studio.

**Matt:**   Man I had no idea.

**David:**   Drink?

**Shannon:**   Oh no. Thanks.

**David:**   Something up?

**Caption:**   Yes

**Shannon:**   No. Thought I heard voices. I'm going to bed.

**David:**  Sure?

**Shannon:**  Talk to you tomorrow.

**Matt:**  Nice to meet you.

**Shannon:**  You too.

*Shannon exits.*

**Matt:**  She's sexy.

**David:**  She has a dick.

**Matt:**  What?

**David:**  He was born a man but believes there's a woman's soul in his body and he's spent his entire adult life trying to let her out.

**Matt:**  Really?

**David:**  He's nearly through the change. He's had hormones, electrolysis, cosmetic surgery — cheek bones, Adam's apple — fairy dust. Everything.

**Matt:**  No way.

**David:**  Way. They make you live as a woman for fucking ever before they'll finish the operation.

**Matt:**  She's got a dick?

**David:**  I met him years ago when he was hooking on Third Avenue.

**Matt:**  You mean some of those women down there are guys?

**David:**   Stay with the tour.

**Matt:**   Fuck.

**David:**   I ran into him again when we were working for this escort agency. He'd just got his tits.

**Matt:**   What kinda life've you had?

**David:**   You don't wanna know.

**Matt:**   So when does Shannon get a twat?

**David:**   He doesn't.

**Matt:**   Why not?

**David:**   Shannon tested hiv plus [HIV positive] six years ago. His lover died of it last year. They don't recommend surgery that major for folks with the virus.

**Matt:**   You positive?

**David:**   I live my life like I were.

**Matt:**   I don't know anyone who has it yet.

**David:**   You will.

**Matt:**   Can you get it from sucking cock?

**David:**   I haven't.

**Matt:**   What were you gonna show me?

**David:**   A painting.

**Matt:**   Excellent.

**David:**   It's not done. But close.

**Matt:**   This it?

*Matt moves to the canvas to pull the cover away. David gets to the canvas first and holds the cover down.*

**David:**   I have to unveil it.

**Matt:**   Sure.

**David:**   I don't want you to get weird about this. I paint a lot of stuff and it's always got a certain kwa *[as in j'e ne c'est quoi]* to it. Not everyone likes my stuff.

**Matt:**   I'll love your stuff.

*David pulls the sheet from the canvas. The audience never sees the painting. Matt stares at the canvas for a long moment.*

**Caption:**   Me

**Matt:**   *Husky.* Jeez. I. It's. Hey.

**Caption:**   Me Me

**David:**   Like it?

**Caption:**   Me Me Me

**Matt:**   No, yeah . . . it's . . . shit, man — you're really good.

**David:**   Thanks.

**Matt:**   You could do this for a living.

**David:**   Actually — I do.

**Caption:**   The Flash

**Matt:**   You're like rich, right?

**David:**   Moderately.

**Matt:**   Are you famous?

**David:**   Kinda.

**Matt:**   What the fuck are you doing at my restaurant?

**David:**   I wanted a job.

**Matt:**   Is that how you see me?

**David:**   Yes.

**Matt:**   I'm beautiful.

**David:**   Yes.

**Matt:**   Who are you?

**David:**   Clark Kent.

**Matt:**   Why'd you paint me naked with the phone?

**David:**   It's about reaching out.

**Matt:**   When're you gonna finish the body?

*David moves to his drug box on the windowledge.*

**David:**   Joint?

**Matt:**   What?

**David:** Skunk, black hash, blonde hash, Quaaludes, coke, half a hit of acid. Two Percodan. Ativan. I think I've got a hit of Xstasy somewhere.

**Matt:** You have coke?

**David:** We could snort some — if you want to make your cock shrivel up and your breath really bad.

**Matt:** I guess one line . . .

**David:** Sure.

**Caption:** Waiting

*Violet falls asleep in front of the television. The Canadian national anthem plays from the television. The music becomes frenetic and distorted — rapid scratch mix — reflecting Matt and David's stoned state.*

**Caption:** Buzzed

**Matt:** When I was a kid I had this friend we usta beat off together and shit but that doesn't mean any-thing right it doesn't mean anything when you're kids. Your painting . . . my cock got chubby while I was looking at it. What the fuck does that mean? It's a painting. Of me.

**David:** More coke?

**Matt:** Just a bit.

**Caption:** Ending Beginning

*Shannon sits in bed wearing a flannel nightgown.*

**Shannon:**   Felt it start. Moving in my system. Faster now. Microscopic things exploding like oranges on the subatomic level. Cells being attacked. War's been declared. Dark armies streaming out of my lymph nodes and into my blood stream. It's started.

*The studio. Matt stands looking at the painting.*

**David:**   Is it you?

**Matt:**   Completely. How can you do that?

**David:**   Telepathy.

**Matt:**   Yeah?

**David:**   You ever dreamed about sucking my cock?

**Matt:**   Yeah.

**David:**   Good.

**Caption:**   What

*David moves to Matt and puts his hands on Matt's shoulders.*

**Caption:**   Am

*Matt puts his hands on David's. They both stare at the painting.*

**Caption:**   I

*Matt turns slowly to face David.*

**Caption:**   Doing

**Matt:**   Oh man . . .

*David and Matt stare at one another, their faces very close together.*

**David:** You've got real bad breath.

**Matt:** So do you.

*Matt puts his arms over David's shoulders and leans against him.*

**David:** I'm too stoned for sex but if you want to sleep for a while and just hold each other I'd really like that.

*Matt leans against David's chest, stoned and drunk.*

**Matt:** Uh humm.

*Matt and David stumble to the bed, still hanging onto each other. A light rises on Kryla by herself. As she speaks, Matt and David undress each other and get into bed.*

**Caption:** Superman

**Kryla:** The last surviving member of his race. A small deco rocket ship hurtling away from the exploding planet of Krypton. His tearful parents watching the rocket disappear into the sky as their world crumbles around them. Cities shatter. Continents crack and heave. Oceans boil. An entire planet — an entire culture — an entire people wiped out by some unforeseen, capricious trick of nature — except for this infant boy streaking toward Earth. Alone. Unprotected. His only chance of something resembling a normal life depends on his ability to integrate with us patently inferior Earthlings. What a very male story.

**Caption:** Skin

*David and Matt are now in bed, under the covers.*

**David:** Didn't think I'd be able to get a hard on.

**Matt:** Me either.

**David:** Like that? *[do you?]*

**Matt:** Uh hunh.

*David rolls on top of Matt. They kiss deep and wet.*

**Matt:** Uhnn.

**David:** Oh yeah.

**Matt:** I am straight.

**David:** I don't mind.

*Violet wakes with a start.*

**Violet:** Matt?

*Brisk fade to black.*

**Caption:** Intermission

Kent Staines as David and Jill Dyck as Kryla. *Photo: Ed Ellis*

**Caption:** Why People Cheat On Their Lovers

*A light on Matt.*

**Matt:** They're bored.

*A light on Kryla.*

**Kryla:** Their delicate egos need boosting.

*A light on David.*

**David:** They can't help themselves.

*A light on Violet.*

**Violet:** They're men.

*A light on Shannon.*

**Shannon:** Cheating's a relative concept. Tom fucked other people all the time. But he was completely up-front about it and — once I got over those suck ass morals our lying, cheating parents foisted on us — I realized his other sexual partners had nothing to do with his love for me. It was okay. It was great. Christians are liars.

**Caption:** Too Late

*Matt enters the bedroom. Violet is waiting for him.*

**Violet:** One day my old man just didn't come home

after work. That was it. Like he disappeared or something. Later we heard he shacked up with some Métis broad in Merritt, B.C.

**Matt:**  I went to David's for a drink. That's it.

**Violet:**  It's six o'clock in the morning asshole!

**Matt:**  I thought you'd be asleep.

**Violet:**  I was. Then I woke up and realized you weren't here. Do you know what that feels like?

**Matt:**  Yeah. We both did it for a lotta years before we met.

**Violet:**  I don't like it!

**Matt:**  I shoulda called.

**Violet:**  Fucking rights you shoulda. I was worried.

**Matt:**  Honey, sometimes I just have to have some time on my own.

**Violet:**  Weren't exactly alone with David.

**Matt:**  You know what I mean.

**Violet:**  Without me.

**Matt:**  The world's not going to end if we spend a little time away from each other.

**Violet:**  Went up to David's?

**Matt:**  He had this painting he wanted me to see.

**Violet:**  Didn't know he painted.

**Matt:** He's pretty good.

**Violet:** You're sweaty.

**Matt:** Walked home.

**Violet:** You okay?

**Matt:** I'm fine. Just don't touch me.

**Violet:** You high?

**Matt:** A bit.

**Violet:** On what?

**Matt:** Pot. But I think it was dusted with something or something. I don't feel so good.

**Violet:** Lay down.

**Matt:** Yeah.

*Matt lies down. Violet sits next to him.*

**Violet:** I'm being too possessive right?

**Matt:** Don't worry about it.

**Violet:** At least you're honest with me. And it's not like I have to worry or anything.

**Matt:** About what?

**Violet:** You hanging out with David. It's not like you're gonna be meeting a lot of other women when you're out with a fag. Right?

**Matt:** Right. I'm gonna shower.

*Matt exits to the bathroom.*

**Caption:**   Intruder

*David smokes a joint and paints madly as he sings triumphant-
ly the first few lines from "I Feel Pretty" from West Side Story.
Kryla enters without knocking. She carries a half-full martini
glass.*

**Kryla:**   If you don't start locking your doors someone is
going to creep in here one night and kill both of
you.

**David:**   Or I could be accosted by a drunk newspaper-
woman while I'm working.

**Kryla:**   The mystery date took me to The Bank after
dinner. Can you imagine? I had pubic hair before
most of the patrons were born. Not that he was
intentionally trying to humiliate me of course. He
honestly thought going to a loud disco filled with
teenagers stoned on Intimacy . . .

**David:**   Xstasy.

**Kryla:**   . . . Whatever . . . would be a perfect place for us
to get to know one another. Naturally I started to
sweat the minute I walked in. I always do. It was
full of smoke. Everyone was drunk and the music
was so loud my diaphragm was vibrating. I'm not
kidding. Saw your lights on and here I am. That is
an alarmingly beautiful painting. Jesus. David —
that's wonderful. Why are you smiling like that?
Isn't this . . . yes it is the guy from the restaurant.
It's the married guy from the restaurant. You're
painting the married guy from the restaurant!

**David:** Wanna toke?

**Kryla:** And you've got an almost maniacal cast to your features that I haven't seen since — what was his name? . . .

**David:** Randy.

**Kryla:** I can never keep them straight. You're in and out of love so quick.

**David:** It's not me that keeps falling out of love.

**Kryla:** Then you admit you're in love with the married guy.

**David:** I admit nothing and his name's Matt.

**Kryla:** You haven't slept with him have you?

**Caption:** Lie

**David:** No.

**Kryla:** You must never do it. No matter how much you want to. He is a *(very loud)* MARRIED man. He has a wife. Is he a fag? Do you think he's a fag? God I hate it when women marry fags. It's so . . . insidious. Is he in love with you? Is he?

**David:** No. And he's not a fag.

**Kryla:** You don't fool me. I hate it when men fall in love with each other. It's so much easier for them. All that shit that drives women crazy makes perfect sense to them.

**David:** Enough.

**Kryla:** Don't fall in love with him. You know we're supposed to grow old and support one another because neither of us has anyone else. If you marry and I don't I'll be full of resentment.

*Shannon enters.*

**Shannon:** Is this a party?

**Kryla:** David has fallen in love with a married man.

**David:** I have not!

**Kryla:** Just look at this painting.

**Shannon:** My dears!

**Kryla:** Now look me in the eye and tell me he is not in love with his subject.

**Shannon:** So what if he is? Look at the painting.

**Kryla:** Sure. As long as it's confined to the painting — but you know as well as I do that when Mr. Love That Dares Not Speak Its Name here gets a hard-on for someone it's impossible to stop him.

**Shannon:** He knows what he's getting into.

**Kryla:** I hate you.

**Shannon:** Why?

**Kryla:** You're practical and you've lost weight.
[*a genuine compliment*]

**Shannon:** *Referring to painting, to David.* Got any mora these building?

**David:**  About six. All that size.

**Shannon:**  Could be major.

**David:**  Definitely.

**Shannon:**  Good for you.

**Kryla:**  I guess the waiting thing was what you needed after all.

**David:**  Yep.

**Kryla:**  Of course you'll quit now. I mean you've got what you wanted, right? Pull out before it gets messy.

**Shannon:**  How many times have you said that very thing?

**David:**  Countless.

**Kryla:**  You're both perverts.

**Shannon:**  *Brooklyn accent.* Me and Velma ain't perverts.

**Kryla:**  And is Mister Married Guy aware you're painting him?

**David:**  Yes.

**Kryla:**  And what about Missus Married Guy?

**Caption:**  Violet

**Kryla:**  Will you have them both to the opening?

**David:**  Who says there'll be an opening?

**Kryla:** It would be criminal for you to paint something that brilliant and not show it.

**David:** I'm painting. That's all that matters.

**Kryla:** *Skeptical.* Right.

**David:** Time for everyone to go home.

**Kryla:** It's the shank of the evening.

**Shannon:** It's half past four.

**David:** Good night.

**Kryla:** Mean ya.

**David:** Love it.

*Kryla exits.*

**Caption:** Beware Beware

**Shannon:** She does have a point.

**David:** I am more than fucking aware of that.

**Shannon:** Straight people and gay people. Too Michael Jackson Lisa Marie Presley.

**David:** It's okay.

**Shannon:** David, you're overdue for another show.

**David:** No, Shan — I'm overdue for another life.

**Shannon:** What's that mean?

**David:** I don't know. I just ... wish I was someone else.

Not someone else. Me. But more me. Different
me. Whatever. It's the painting that counts. Not
the showings. He makes me want to paint him —
capture him. Understand him.

**Shannon:** Be him?

**Caption:** Normal

**David:** Sometimes.

**Caption:** Tell Him

**Shannon:** David?

**David:** Huh?

**Shannon:** There was blood in my shit today.

**David:** Jesus.

**Caption:** Have I Changed

*Their bedroom. Matt stands naked in front of the full-length
mirror examining himself. Violet enters and watches him for
a moment.*

**Violet:** What the fuck are you doing?

**Matt:** Nothing.

**Violet:** You're worse than a woman. Come to bed.

*Matt gets into bed. Violet snuggles up to him.*

**Violet:** You smell funny.

**Matt:** No I don't.

*Violet moves under the covers, going down on Matt. He puts his hands behind his head and closes his eyes very tight.*

**Caption:**   (David)

*Day. David is working on another canvas. The first one leans against the wall, covered. Kryla is there.*

**Kryla:**   This is absolutely the last mention.

**David:**   Let's hear it.

**Kryla:**   It's not major. I don't want to appear retarded.

**David:**   Let's hear it.

**Kryla:**   So not only does the Bridgeland strip feature some of the city's most interesting antique and second-hand shops and such happening eateries as Nineteen Twelve and *(very loud )* THE MONTERAY DINER, it is now home to Calgary's newest live theatre.

**David:**   Good. Subtle. Like it. Thanks.

**Kryla:**   Another one?

**David:**   Can't stop.

**Kryla:**   Sometimes I feel like you're becoming someone I don't know.

**David:**   Me too.

**Caption:**   Cancer

*The restaurant. Matt is sweeping the restaurant. Shannon enters. Shannon ignores Matt, looking very depressed, and takes a seat. Matt moves to the table.*

**Matt:**   Hi.

**Shannon:**   How are you?

**Matt:**   Fine. Good. You're . . . um . . . my wife's in the kitchen. . . .

**Shannon:**   Yeah?

**Matt:**   I she do you want a coffee?

**Shannon:**   This has something to do with you being over last night.

**Matt:**   No yeah it's okay. Really.

*Violet enters from the kitchen.*

**Violet:**   Matt, where's the tomato paste?

**Matt:**   Top shelf. Behind the olive oil.

**Violet:**   Hi.

**Shannon:**   Hi.

**Violet:**   You been crying?

**Shannon:**   No.

**Matt:**   This is Shannon. Friend of David's.

**Violet:**   You should fix your eyes.

**Shannon:**   Roommate.

**Violet:**   What?

**Shannon:**   David and I. We live together.

**Violet:**   I didn't know he lived with someone.

**Matt:**   Neither did I.

*David enters.*

**David:**   What is this? A reunion? Violet did you meet . . .

**Violet:**   *Cutting him off.* Just now.

**David:**   What'd the doctor say?

**Shannon:**   Nothing.

**Violet:**   Behind the olive oil?

**Matt:**   Yep.

*Violet exits. Matt moves behind the bar.*

**David:**   Nothing?

**Shannon:**   We'll talk at home.

**David:**   Okay.

**Shannon:**   Later.

**David:**   Bye.

*Shannon exits.*

**Matt:**   She okay?

**David:**   I don't know.

**Caption:**   Last Night

**Matt:**   Smoking or non?

**David:** Whatever.

**Matt:** Your pick.

**David:** Is this gonna be weird now because if it is just let me know. I've done the weird ride and it makes me sick.

**Matt:** I feel sorta weird.

**David:** Me too.

*Violet enters from the kitchen.*

**Violet:** How many resos we got?

**Matt:** Thirty.

**Violet:** David, I couldn't reach the tomato paste. Could you grab me a coupla cans?

**David:** No prob.

*David exits.*

**Violet:** I didn't know he was living with a woman.

**Matt:** She's a man.

**Violet:** What?

**Matt:** Transvestite. Soul of a woman in the body of a man.

**Violet:** Oh.

**Caption:** Freak

**Matt:** She has AIDS.

**Violet:** Big surprise.

*David enters with two cans of tomato paste.*

**David:** Here.

**Violet:** Thanks.

*Violet takes the cans from David and exits to the kitchen. David and Matt check their tables as they speak. They do not make eye contact at all.*

**Matt:** Shannon being here was weird.

**David:** She doesn't know anything except that you were over.

**Matt:** Calgary's small.

**David:** Practically a village. Did you hate it?

**Matt:** No. I was there man. I was there. I love Violet. That painting. I'm fucked.

**David:** Then let's make sure it doesn't happen again.

**Matt:** You wouldn't mind?

**David:** Not if it's gonna fuck you up.

**Matt:** Really?

**David:** Really.

**Matt:** Thank you.

**Caption:** Girltalk

*Kryla and Shannon are in the studio.*

**Kryla:** Phone sex. She makes a fortune. Good interview too. And she told me that the number one fantasy — the number one fantasy the men that call want to talk about is ... is ... guess ...

**Shannon:** Sucking cock.

**Kryla:** Yes! Can you believe it. She said usually there was a woman involved but — well — sucking cock is sucking cock isn't it?

**Shannon:** What was number two?

**Kryla:** Tying women up.

**Shannon:** Aren't they predictable

**Kryla:** Worse than Edmonton. *[rival city in Alberta]*

*Shannon exits.*

**Caption:** Early Influences

*The studio. David is painting.*

**Kryla:** Who's the figure behind Matt?

**David:** My cousin, Wally.

**Kryla:** The older one that fucked you when you were a kid?

**David:** Mmm.

**Kryla:** Isn't that an interesting parallel.

**David:** Mmm hmm.

**Kryla:**  You come from a totally dysfunctional background.

**David:**  Who doesn't?

**Kryla:**  Are you seeing someone?

**David:**  What gives you that idea?

**Kryla:**  I never see you anymore unless you're painting.

**David:**  It's all I've been doing.

**Kryla:**  So I'm forced to go out on my own yet again?

**David:**  Take Shannon.

**Kryla:**  She won't drink anymore.

**David:**  Sorry.

**Kryla:**  Love me.

**David:**  Mean ya.

*Kryla exits. David paints, very into it. Shannon enters.*

**Shannon:**  I have seen the face of horror and it is Betty Rubble.

**David:**  What?

**Shannon:**  Cancer.

**David:**  Fuck.

*David stops painting. They look at one another for a long moment.*

**Shannon:** On my ass and my legs. KS. *[Karposi's Sarcoma]* Maybe internally as well.

**David:** Fuck.

**Shannon:** The AZT's not working. The DDI's too toxic. I have to go into chemo next week.

**Caption:** Contact

*David hugs Shannon.*

**Shannon:** I don't mind dying but I don't want to be ugly while it's happening.

**David:** What did Doctor Thingface say?

**Shannon:** My T-cell count is nonexistent. He suggested that if there's anything I really want to do that I haven't done already I should think about doing it now.

**David:** Excellent.

**Caption:** Why Not You

*David rolls a joint as they speak.*

**Shannon:** You were as slutty as the rest of us.

**David:** Lucky.

**Shannon:** You didn't get fucked.

**David:** Honey, I can't even shit big.

**Shannon:** Or maybe you just couldn't open up enough to let someone else inside you.

**David:**   That's possible.

**Shannon:**   It's not fair.

**David:**   Shan, we're all living with it — even if we're not infected.

*Shannon examines the canvas as they share a joint.*

**Shannon:**   Isn't that your child-molester cousin in the background?

**David:**   You know everything.

**Shannon:**   Did you ever hear from him after that interview you did about child abuse and incest?

**David:**   My grandmother wrote me a letter suggesting the entire thing was my fault because I was a homosexual and liked it. At three.

**Shannon:**   Bother you?

**David:**   Not for years.

**Shannon:**   They're your family.

**David:**   You're my family. Shannon, I'm falling in love.

**Shannon:**   Thought that was over.

**David:**   I don't want it to be.

**Shannon:**   What are you going to do?

**David:**   Callously and craftily weasel him back into my bed.

**Shannon:**   Oh please — you sound like Faye Dunaway.

**David:** I really like this guy and I know he really likes me.

**Shannon:** Maybe fag and lesbian aren't nouns. Maybe they're verbs.

**David:** Do you think if I like concentrate real hard and send out mega alpha waves I can make him come here to me?

**Shannon:** Sure.

**Caption:** The Revelation

*Matt and Violet sit at a table having coffee before opening the restaurant. Violet is reading the newspaper.*

**Violet:** He's gonna tell her who he really is.

**Matt:** What?

**Violet:** Superman. Says here he's gonna tell Lois his real identity.

**Matt:** No way.

**Violet:** What it says.

*Violet hands Matt the paper. He scans the article quickly.*

**Violet:** I thought that secret identity thing was a totally big deal.

**Matt:** It was.

*David enters for work.*

**Violet:** Yo, Wonder Boy.

**David:** Hi, Violet.

**Matt:** Superman's gonna tell Lois who he really is.

**David:** I heard.

**Matt:** Pretty radical.

**David:** Makes sense. How long can you keep a secret like that?

**Violet:** I always thought it was kinda weird she never figured it out. I mean a pair of glasses and everyone's fooled? Women in love see better than that.

*The telephone rings. Matt moves to the kitchen to answer it.*

**Matt:** Got it.

*Matt exits.*

**Violet:** David? . . .

**David:** Yeah?

**Violet:** You know what's wrong with Matt?

**David:** What makes you think there's something wrong?

**Violet:** He's got something on his mind.

**David:** You know him better than I do.

**Violet:** I know. But men talk to each other sometimes.

**David:** Sure.

**Violet:**   I thought he mighta said something or something.

**David:**   No.

*Matt enters.*

**Violet:**   Reso?

**Matt:**   Party of twelve.

**Violet:**   All right.

**Caption:**   Noble Sacrifice

**David:**   I'm giving my notice today.

**Matt:**   What?

**Violet:**   Really?

**David:**   I'll stay 'til you find someone else.

**Violet:**   Why?

**David:**   I've got other work to do now.

**Violet:**   We'll miss you.

**David:**   I'll still drop by.

**Violet:**   You sure?

**David:**   Yeah.

**Violet:**   I've got sauces to make. *To Matt.* Talk him out of it.

*Violet exits.*

**David:** It's too Jackie Collins *[glitzy authoress]* — even for me.

**Matt:** We wouldn't do anything here.

**David:** Violet's not stupid.

**Matt:** Why would she think anything's going on?

**David:** I can't lie. You can give the job to someone who really needs it.

**Matt:** We'll never see each other.

**David:** We will if you want to.

**Matt:** I'm always fucking here.

**David:** You can see me after work.

**Matt:** It won't be the same.

**David:** No.

*Kryla in the studio.*

**Kryla:** It's a good decision. You got everything you needed out of that place anyway.

**David:** I don't really want to discuss it.

**Kryla:** Aren't we surly.

**David:** Go home, Kryla.

**Kryla:** Are you kicking me out because I'm saying things you don't want to hear?

**David:**  I'm kicking you out because I have work to do and I want to be alone.

**Kryla:**  All right then.

*Kryla exits.*

**Caption:**  Two Weeks Later

*The restaurant. It is closed. Matt is nursing a beer. Violet sits with him.*

**Violet:**  I like Bess. It's nice to have another woman around the place.

**Matt:**  Yeah.

**Violet:**  Look, I know she's not David.

**Matt:**  It's just not the same.

**Violet:**  Why don't you go see him?

**Matt:**  When do I have time?

**Violet:**  Right now.

**Matt:**  You don't mind?

**Violet:**  Not if it makes you happy.

*Matt takes Violet's hand.*

**Matt:**  You're great.

**Violet:**  I know.

*David sits in the studio staring at a new, blank canvas. He is smoking a joint and drinking a vodka. Shannon enters with a bag.*

**Shannon:**   Pigtits.

**David:**   Cowcunt.

**Shannon:**   Got you something.

**David:**   What?

*Shannon pulls a comic book from the bag.*

**Shannon:**   Action Comics number six-sixty-two. Superman reveals all to Lois. Do you know they're selling for five bucks now? I couldn't believe it. It's only been out for a month and a half. I remember when comics were twelve cents. And when did comic fans gets so scary? Those kids masturbate too much. You can just tell.

**David:**   *Examining comic.* Since when does Lois Lane have brown hair?

**Shannon:**   Got me.

**David:**   Thanks, Shan.

**Shannon:**   Why don't you just call him?

**David:**   Who?

**Shannon:**   Fuck off.

**David:**   It's better this way.

**Shannon:**   Being miserable? Not painting?

**David:** Toke?

**Shannon:** Sure. Helps with the nausea. Can you notice my hair's falling out?

**David:** No.

**Shannon:** Am I developing those dark circles under my eyes and that emaciated look that lets you know someone's dying?

**Caption:** Yes

**David:** No.

**Shannon:** I'm so fucking tired.

**David:** I feel the same way. It's called over thirty.

**Shannon:** Don't minimize this.

**David:** A safe could fall on me tomorrow. I could be hit by a car. My plane could crash. I could have an aneurism. Being sick doesn't necessarily mean you're gonna kick before everyone else you know.

**Shannon:** Do you love me?

**David:** Yes.

**Shannon:** If they can't do anything about this I'm bailing offa the AIDS train when I want to.

**Caption:** Suicide

**Shannon:** I'll need some support.

**David:** We don't need to discuss this now.

**Shannon:**   I think we do.

**David:**   You're gonna be fine . . .

**Shannon:**   David I have cancer. I have thrush. I have little white warts growing on my face that the doctor burns off every two weeks. I am not gonna be fine.

**David:**   I can't talk about suicide.

**Shannon:**   Feel sorry for yourself on your own time. I'm the one who's dying.

**David:**   You're dying. I'm living. They're both hard. You kill yourself if you want and go to wherever it is people who kill themselves go to — but I'm not committing to anything until I've given it some real thought because I have to live with myself. I don't get to bow out gracefully.

**Shannon:**   I'd switch places with you in a second.

**David:**   Wouldn't it be great if I could give you some of my life. You know . . . knock ten — fifteen years off the end of my life span so we could extend yours.

**Shannon:**   I don't want you to do anything to help me. I just want to know that if that's the decision I make, I'll have your support.

**David:**   You'll have my support.

**Shannon:**   What can I do for you?

**David:**   *Holding a toke.* Tell me things are gonna change. It's not always going to be like this.

Kent Staines as David. *Photo: Ed Ellis*

**Shannon:** *Holding a toke.* Things are gonna change. It's not always going to be like this.

*The doorbell rings.*

**David:** It's him.

**Shannon:** How do you know?

**David:** X-ray vision.

**Shannon:** Or alpha wave delay.

*David opens the door. Matt is there.*

**David:** C'min.

*Matt enters.*

**Matt:** Hi.

**Shannon:** Nice to see you.

**Matt:** You too.

**Shannon:** Excuse me.

**David:** Need anything?

**Shannon:** A time machine.

**David:** I'll work on it.

**Shannon:** Fab. 'night boys.

**Matt:** 'night.

*Shannon exits.*

**David:** I've thought about you a lot.

**Matt:** I'm not queer.

**David:** Then why come back?

**Matt:** I don't know who I am anymore. What I feel. I like women. I've always liked women. I've never wanted to do anything weird except when I was like sorta attracted to my sister at thirteen. But I never did anything.

**David:** Everyone's attracted to their sister at thirteen.

**Matt:** But there's something about you — the things you say — the way you look at me — make me feel — these paintings — what you see — and I don't know what I want but the maybe we could just be friends? Can we just be friends?

**David:** What do you want?

**Matt:** To be with you.

**David:** When it's convenient.

**Matt:** When I can.

**David:** What about cheating on Violet?

**Matt:** This is different.

**David:** How?

**Matt:** You're a man.

**David:** I don't believe all relationships are the same. I don't believe this man woman thing is the only way to live. I don't think we have to love only one person. I don't think monogamy is a natural thing for all people. I think love needs to be redefined.

**Caption:** Love

**Matt:** Why don't I feel the way I'm supposed to feel?

**David:** Because eighty percent of everything our parents taught us is wrong. The other twenty percent is immoral.

**Matt:** I can't stand the thought of anyone finding out.

**David:** Ashamed?

**Matt:** Scared.

**David:** We all feel that way.

**Matt:** You never show it.

**David:** I've been doing it for a long time.

**Matt:** It's the fag thing. Queer. Pansy. Sissy.

**David:** They're only words.

**Matt:** People hate you.

**David:** Not everyone.

**Matt:** It makes everything so hard.

**David:** That's not necessarily a disadvantage.

**Matt:** No?

**David:** Adversity can create very clear goals.

**Matt:** It's I just want to know another guy — not feel so alone.

**David:** Me too.

**Caption:** Expose

*Matt takes his shirt off.*

**Matt:** I feel like my skin knows your skin.

*David removes his shirt.*

**Matt:** Like your body's calling out to mine.

*David undoes his pants and pushes them down to his knees.*

**Matt:** I can smell you on me after we've been together. I catch whiffs of you at the stupidest times. Getting coffee. Changing a tape.

*David steps out of his pants and pulls his socks off.*

**Matt:** And it's not even like I'm into cocks or whatever. It's just you.

*David removes his underwear, standing naked before Matt. Matt stares at him.*

**Caption:** Blood rushes

*Matt undoes his pants slowly and pulls them down, still looking at David.*

**Matt:** And I don't know.

**Caption:** Swelling

**Matt:** Can't control it.

**Caption:**  Growing

**Matt:**  Doesn't it bother you knowing I sleep with Violet too?

**Caption:**  Yes

**David:**  You're not the only person I sleep with.

**Matt:**  No?

**David:**  No.

*David moves to Matt and runs his hands up the sides of Matt's body.*

**David:**  You're warm. Smooth.

*David moves behind Matt and puts his arms around him, pulling Matt in tight to his body.*

**David:**  Hard.

**Matt:**  Ohhh.

*David slides Matt's shorts down from behind. They stop at Matt's knees.*

**David:**  I love you.

**Matt:**  You'd never show those paintings would you? I mean to the public.

**David:**  Not if you didn't want me to.

**Matt:**  I love you too.

*David handles Matt's cock and balls from behind. They kiss*

*passionately. A light rises on Violet in bed. She is speaking
to Matt off.*

**Caption:**   Fucking Men

**Violet:**   Don't forget to lift the goddamn toilet seat! I
hate it when you piss all over the toilet seat.

*Sound of a toilet flushing. Matt enters, naked, and climbs into
bed as they speak.*

**Matt:**   I'm not eleven years old.

**Violet:**   No. But you still piss on the toilet seat sometimes. How's David?

**Matt:**   Busy.

**Violet:**   Maybe the three of us could do something
sometime.

**Caption:**   No

**Matt:**   Maybe.

**Violet:**   Play cards or something.

**Matt:**   Maybe.

*The studio. David is painting.*

**Kryla:**   Who's the faceless woman behind your pederast
cousin?

**Caption:**   Violet

**David:**   No one.

Kryla:  Why's she got Helen Keller glasses on?

David:  So she can answer the iron.

Kryla:  I hear the restaurant's become quite the trendy hangout.

David:  That's the rumour.

Kryla:  David, do you dislike me?

Caption:  Maybe

*David stops painting and looks at Kryla.*

David:  What makes you ask that?

Kryla:  You never listen to me anymore.

David:  I'm working.

Kryla:  You've got something else on your mind.

David:  Occasionally. Forgive me.

Kryla:  That's it. That's it exactly. Everything you say to me has developed this edge I don't much care for. What are you angry about? Is it me?

David:  Y'know, Kryla, it seems like you're right behind me every time I turn around.

Kryla:  Oh?

David:  I just wish you . . . weren't . . . always around so much.

*Pause.*

**Kryla:** Presto. Your wish is granted.

*Kryla exits. David sits, lighting a joint. He takes a couple of tokes.*

**Caption:** Time Passing

*Matt enters.*

**Matt:** What's wrong?

**David:** Nothing.

**Matt:** Sure?

**David:** Yep.

*Matt puts his arms around David.*

**Matt:** You're great.

**David:** I know. Wanna go to a bar?

**Matt:** Gay bar?

**David:** Yeah.

**Matt:** Let's just go to bed.

**David:** I need a beer.

**Matt:** I won't be able to come back.

**David:** Do we have to have sex every time we get together?

**Matt:** Yes.

**Caption:**   Our Vocabulary

*Shannon lies in bed. Kryla sits with her.*

**Kryla:**   Diana Rigg in The Avengers. She was the best. Those leather jump suits. I loved her.

**Shannon:**   Linda Carter as Wonder Woman. I used to pray to Satan to make me into Linda Carter.

**Kryla:**   David's mad at me.

**Shannon:**   Why?

**Kryla:**   Sticking my nose where it doesn't belong.

**Shannon:**   Sounds justified.

**Kryla:**   I've been sticking my nose in his business for twenty years. Suddenly it's a problem?

**Shannon:**   He's going through something.

**Kryla:**   What?

**Shannon:**   He's learning he can't leap tall buildings in a single bound.

**Kryla:**   He's just learning that now?

**Shannon:**   Men.

**Caption:**   Fucking Men

*Matt and David are in bed, partially under the covers. Matt is putting on a condom.*

**David:**   Got it on?

**Matt:**   Yeah.

**David:**   Okay.

**Matt:**   Slow.

**David:**   Yeah. Just the head. Okay.

**Matt:**   I'm not hurting you?

**David:**   It's not that big.

**Matt:**   Funny funny.

**David:**   Okay . . . easy . . . easy. Wait. Pull out pull out.

**Matt:**   Okay?

**David:**   Yeah. Just a little slower.

**Matt:**   Like that?

**David:**   Yeah.

**Matt:**   Okay?

**David:**   Yeah.

**Matt:**   This is great.

**David:**   Yeah.

**Caption:**   Connected

*A spot on Violet.*

**Violet:**   If there was just a way we could climb into each other's skin.

*A light on Kryla.*

**Kryla:**   Read each other's minds.

*A spot on Shannon.*

**Shannon:**   Be absolutely sure we're not the only ones
thinking this way.

**Violet:**   Then we'd know.

**Kryla:**   Then we'd be sure.

**Shannon:**   Then we'd understand.

**Caption:**   The Talk

*David and Matt are in bed. David is rolling a joint.*

**David:**   And where exactly do you see this heading?

**Matt:**   Haven't thought about it. Where do you see it
heading?

**David:**   *Shrugs.* Wherever.

**Matt:**   Does it bother you I'm with someone else?

**David:**   Sometimes.

**Matt:**   Don't you want to meet a guy you could live
with . . . you know . . . settle down with?

**Caption:**   Lie

**David:**   I don't care.

**Matt:**   Don't you get tired of being alone so much?

**David:**   I have Shannon. Kryla.

**Matt:**   How is Shan?

**David:**   Not well.

**Matt:**   Man, that is such a drag.

**David:**   That's one way of putting it.

**Matt:**   How do you deal with all this, David?

**David:**   I drink too much, smoke my brains out, quaff
Ativan like jelly beans and try not to think about it.

**Matt:**   What is it with you?

**David:**   What?

**Matt:**   You're not like a straight guy and you're not really like a gay guy either.

**David:**   I'm a mutant.

**Matt:**   What's your mutant power?

**David:**   The ability to make my cock hard and come
whenever I want to.

**Matt:**   Great power.

**David:**   Why don't you let me fuck you now?

**Caption:**   NO!

**Matt:**   I don't think so.

**David:**   It's okay. Really.

**Matt:**   It's not I've never even fantasized about that.

**David:**   I hardly think I should be penalized for your lack of imagination. And you've got a wonderful ass. . . .

**Matt:**   I couldn't.

**David:**   You might surprise yourself.

**Matt:**   I don't want to surprise myself.

*David pounces on Matt, wrestling with him playfully. Matt is into it initially.*

**David:**   Then I'll just have to take you by force.

**Matt:**   Gedouda here!

**David:**   Throw you down on the pavement and fuck you hard like a dog.

**Matt:**   No.

*David is getting the best of Matt. He starts to turn him over on his stomach.*

**David:**   Submit submit! You can't avoid my will!

*Matt suddenly hits David in the face.*

**Matt:**   No!

*David gets out of bed, holding his nose.*

**Matt:**   David . . . I'm sorry.

**David:**   My fault.

**Matt:**   Your lip's bleeding.

**David:**   I'm okay.

**Matt:**   I'm really really sorry.

**David:**   It's okay. Everyone's got their limits.

**Matt:**   Guess we just reached mine.

**David:**   You ever hit Violet?

**Matt:**   No way. I'd never hit a woman. I'd never would've hit you. You scared me.

**David:**   Don't worry about it.

*Matt kisses David.*

**Matt:**   I'm sorry.

**David:**   Stop apologizing.

*Matt runs his hands over David's body.*

**Matt:**   I don't wanna hurt you. I don't wanna hurt anyone.

**David:**   No?

**Matt:**   No.

*Matt leads David back to bed, stroking him.*

**Matt:**   Forgive me?

**David:**   You love me?

**Matt:**   Sure.

**David:**   Then I forgive you.

*They kiss. Matt jerks off David beneath the covers.*

**Matt:**   But I can't let you fuck me. Just can't.

**David:**   I got that.

**Matt:**   And I'll never leave my wife for you.

**David:**   I didn't expect you would.

**Matt:**   I can't.

*Matt disappears beneath the covers, sucking David's cock.*

**Caption:**   He's Not the One.

*The door to the studio opens. Kryla enters.*

**Kryla:**   Darling I absolutely must have an anti —

*She sees them. Matt looks up from beneath the covers, shocked.*

**Kryla:**   Oh for God's sake.

**David:**   Kryla.

**Kryla:**   You might at least have the decency to lock the door.

**David:**   This is my house.

**Kryla:**   You're fucking married.

**David:**   Get out.

146 / POOR SUPER MAN

**Kryla:** What'd you tell your wife? You're out with the boys? Watching the hockey game?

**David:** Get out!

**Kryla:** She doesn't know — does she? She trusts you. She believes in you. What would she say if she found out? What would she say if someone told her?

**Matt:** Please. . . .

**Kryla:** Your best friend's dying in the next room and you're in here with some straight guy!

**David:** Kryla, come on . . .

**Kryla:** You're a fucking liar!

**David:** Kryla . . .

**Kryla:** You guys make me sick.

*Kryla exits quickly. Matt jumps out of bed and begins to dress.*

**David:** Matt . . .

**Matt:** She's gonna tell her.

**David:** No.

**Matt:** She's gonna fucking tell her!

**David:** She's just upset because I lied to her.

**Matt:** Why didn't you lock the fucking door?

**David:** Matt . . .

**Matt:**   I knew this would happen.

**David:**   She'll walk it off. She will. Calm down for a
minute.

**Matt:**   She's going to tell my wife.

**David:**   What if she is? What are you going to do? Stop
her? How? It was gonna happen, Matt. You had to
know that. That's why I left the restaurant. This shit
always gets found out.

**Matt:**   Jesus.

**David:**   Maybe you should tell Violet yourself.

**Caption:**   ?

**David:**   Get everything in the open.

**Matt:**   You're crazy.

**David:**   I didn't realize you were this stressed about it.

**Matt:**   You think I want people saying I'm a fucking
queer?

**David:**   What are you then?

**Matt:**   Outa here. I can't do this anymore.

**David:**   You think you can just walk out of this now?
You think you can just dump me and go on with
your life like this was all a dream sequence or
something?

**Matt:**   Yeah.

**David:**   You're wrong.

**Matt:**   We'll find out.

**David:**   You break up like this and it'll never be over, Matt. You'll think about me all the time. Whenever you're with her I'll be there. I — what we have — this just won't go away because you want it to.

**Matt:**   I can't do it anymore, David.

**David:**   What?

**Matt:**   I don't love you.

**David:**   What?

**Matt:**   I don't know why I said it.

**David:**   Are you serious?

**Matt:**   Yeah. Sorry.

*Matt begins to exit.*

**David:**   Don't.

*Matt stops.*

**Caption:**   Leave

**David:**   Please.

**Caption:**   Stay

**David:**   You're.

**Caption:**   Mine

**David:**   Matt? . . .

**Matt:**   I don't. *[love you]*

*Matt exits. David pulls a sheet around himself very tight.*
*Shannon enters. She has trouble standing erect and holds*
*her butt with one hand.*

**Shannon:**   What're you doing?

**David:**   Having a slow internal nervous breakdown.

**Shannon:**   Why?

**David:**   The man I love just told me he doesn't love me
after my best friend discovered us in bed together
and has threatened to tell the man I love's wife.

**Shannon:**   Girls ruin everything.

*Shannon sits on the ledge with some difficulty.*

**David:**   Should you be up?

**Shannon:**   Every chance I get. I took a shit that just
about killed me.

**David:**   Want me to get your painkillers?

**Shannon:**   Took three.

**David:**   Something to eat?

**Shannon:**   No. I just need to be up.

**David:**   What's all over the side of your robe?

**Shannon:**   What?

**David:**   Stand up. Turn around.

*Shannon stands up and turns around. The ass of the bathrobe she wears is covered with blood.*

**David:**   Jesus, Shannon.

**Shannon:**   What?

**David:**   Didn't you notice?

**Shannon:**   What?

**David:**   Come on. Let's clean you up.

**Shannon:**   *Finally notices the blood.* Oh fuck.

**David:**   Come on.

**Shannon:**   Why didn't I notice?

**Caption:**   After Careful Consideration

*Violet is working on her own, singing to herself. Kryla enters.*

**Kryla:**   Hello.

**Violet:**   Oh hi.

**Kryla:**   Are you closed?

**Violet:**   Pretty much. Yeah.

**Kryla:**   Can I still get a coffee?

**Violet:**   Sure.

*Violet gets the coffee.*

**Kryla:**   Alone?

**Violet:** Yeah. I close for my husband on Thursday nights. Do I know you from somewhere?

**Kryla:** I have a newspaper column.

**Violet:** That's right. You write about us.

**Kryla:** I do.

**Violet:** Nice to meet you. *(Wipes off her hand and offers it to Kryla.)* I'm Violet.

*Kryla takes Violet's hand.*

**Kryla:** Nice to meet you, Violet.

*Kryla continues to hold Violet's hand.*

**Kryla:** It's very nice to meet you.

**Violet:** Do something for you?

**Kryla:** Tell me something.

**Violet:** Sure.

**Kryla:** Are you happy?

**Violet:** What kinda question's that?

**Kryla:** Are you?

**Violet:** Sure.

**Kryla:** Really?

**Violet:** Yeah. Sure.

*Pause.*

**Kryla:**   Good for you.

*Kryla lets go of Violet's hand.*

**Kryla:**   Have a nice night.

*Kryla exits.*

*David is putting Shannon into bed after cleaning her up.*

**Shannon:**   Tired.

**David:**   Go to sleep.

**Shannon:**   Stay?

**David:**   Sure.

**Shannon:**   Do you ever think like maybe you get
involved with these straight guys so you won't
have to risk a committed homosexual relationship?

**David:**   Do you ever think like maybe you're too sick to
play armchair psychologist?

**Shannon:**   Something's happening in my brain, David.
I can feel things kind of moving — melting. I forget
stuff.

**David:**   We'll get it checked out. They'll treat it.

**Shannon:**   What happens when we come to something
that's not treatable?

**David:**   We won't.

**Shannon:**   We will. Soon.

**David:**   How do you know?

**Shannon:** Because I'm bored. I don't know what to do anymore. I've seen it happen in everyone I know. First you're bored, then you die.

**David:** You're not gonna die for a long time.

**Shannon:** You're wrong. You've got to accept it.

**David:** I can't.

**Shannon:** Yes you can.

**David:** I can't imagine life without you.

**Shannon:** You've got to move on.

**David:** I'm scared.

**Shannon:** Me too.

**David:** I have to show those paintings.

**Shannon:** Yeah?

**David:** They tell the truth.

**Shannon:** I'd be scared.

**David:** I'll never see him again.

**Shannon:** He's not like you, David.

**David:** I don't know anyone who's like me. I'm a fucking alien.

**Shannon:** We're all a fucking sideshow. Don't waste time on shit you can't change.

**David:** Bitch.

**Shannon:** Asshole.

**Caption:** Fear

*The restaurant. Violet has just finished cleaning up. Matt enters.*

**Violet:** You're home early?

**Matt:** Yeah.

**Violet:** What's wrong?

**Matt:** Nothing. How was your night?

**Violet:** Great. Busy 'til nine, then zip. Sent Bess home early.

**Matt:** No complaints?

**Violet:** No. Oh . . . that reporter came in.

**Matt:** From the *Herald*?

**Violet:** Yeah.

**Matt:** What for?

**Violet:** I don't know. It was kinda weird.

**Matt:** Weird how?

**Violet:** She wanted to know if I was happy.

**Matt:** Happy?

**Violet:** Yeah. She asked me if I was happy, then she left.

**Matt:** Yeah?

**Violet:** Mebbe she's gonna write about us being happy now.

**Matt:** That's it?

**Violet:** Yeah.

*Matt sits, relieved.*

**Violet:** You happy Matt?

**Matt:** Yeah. I'm happy.

**Caption:** Brain Lesions

*A light rises on Shannon in bed.*

**Shannon:** Bob Seeger! Bob Seeger!

*David enters quickly.*

**David:** Shan?

**Shannon:** You said you'd play it. You said! You said!

**David:** You okay?

**Shannon:** He said he'd play it.

**David:** Who?

**Shannon:** And he didn't. He didn't. He said he would!

**David:** Ssh.

**Shannon:** He promised!

**David:** I know.

**Shannon:**   He said he would!

**David:**   I know. Ssh.

**Caption:**   Three Weeks Later

*Violet is reading the newspaper. Morning. Matt enters in a robe.*

**Matt:**   Coffee on?

**Violet:**   Yeah.

*Matt gets coffee.*

**Violet:**   Guess David's been busy with the show huh?

**Matt:**   What show?

**Violet:**   Some gallery in Kensington. Says right here. A new series by David McMillan.

**Matt:**   Really?

**Violet:**   Pretty good picture of him. Let's go.

*Matt takes the newspaper from Violet.*

**Matt:**   A show?

**Caption:**   A Show

*A light rises on David in the studio. David is surveying six large canvases. The audience sees only the backs of the canvases.*

**David:**   Well of course I'm having a show.

*Matt joins David.*

**Matt:**  What if Violet sees them?

**David:**  What did you think, Matt? That I was just painting these for fun?

**Matt:**  Don't I get some say in what happens to them?

**David:**  No.

**Matt:**  They're of me.

**David:**  You didn't sit for them. You didn't create them.

**Matt:**  I inspired them.

**David:**  You don't pay the fruit when you do a still life.

**Matt:**  You promised you wouldn't do this.

**David:**  I have to.

**Matt:**  People'll think I was your lover.

**David:**  You were my lover.

**Matt:**  Why are you doing this?

**Caption:**  Choose

**David:**  I assumed you understood.

**Matt:**  I don't know anything about this stuff.

**David:**  I have to do it. Take advantage of it. People are gonna be asking about the model. You could be famous.

**Matt:** I don't want to be famous.

**David:** Everyone wants to be famous.

**Matt:** I don't want to be a famous fag!

**David:** You didn't mind when I made your restaurant famous.

**Matt:** This is different.

**David:** You dumped me.

**Matt:** I had no choice.

**David:** Neither do I.

**Matt:** Do you want me to beg?

**David:** Wouldn't make a bit of difference.

**Matt:** You're an asshole!

**David:** I knew we had something besides sex in common.

**Matt:** I'll wreck them. I will. I'll break in . . .

*David grabs Matt.*

**David:** You even think about touching one of these paintings and it won't be your restaurant that'll be in the gossip columns — it'll be stories about you sucking my cock. You got that?

**Matt:** Yeah.

*David lets go of Matt.*

**David:** I have to do this, Matt. For me. Because I can't lie anymore. I'm sorry.

**Matt:** If you want I mean if it'll keep you from showing the paintings I'll come back. Do whatever you like . . .

**Caption:** Illumination

**David:** How did I ever drown in someone so shallow?

**Matt:** David. Please.

**David:** I have to.

**Matt:** Fuck.

*Matt exits. David turns and stares at the paintings. A light rises on Kryla.*

**Kryla:** They're going to kill him.

*A light rises on Shannon.*

**Shannon:** I've already started thinking of myself in the past tense.

**Kryla:** Superman.

**Shannon:** Everything's then. Nothing's now.

**Kryla:** They're going to kill Superman.

**Caption:** Becoming A Man

*The restaurant. Violet sits at a table peeling carrots. Matt enters.*

**Violet:** What?

**Matt:** We have to talk.

**Violet:** 'bout what?

**Matt:** David's show.

**Violet:** Why?

**Matt:** The paintings.

**Violet:** What about 'em?

**Matt:** They're of me.

**Violet:** You?

**Matt:** Nude.

**Violet:** What?

**Matt:** We've been sleeping together.

**Violet:** What?

**Matt:** David and me.

**Violet:** What?!

**Matt:** It's not . . .

**Violet:** You're kidding.

**Matt:** No.

**Violet:** You've been sleeping with David?

**Matt:** Yes.

**Violet:** David our waiter.

**Matt:** We're friends. He's not what I thought. I didn't I love you.

**Violet:** What?

**Matt:** I do love you.

**Violet:** You don't fucking love me.

**Matt:** I do.

**Violet:** You're a fucking fag. I am so fucking stupid. You've always been a fag haven't you? I always thought you were a little feminine. Didn't see it. Didn't fucking see it.

**Matt:** I'm not a fag.

**Violet:** You've been sleeping with another guy. Far as I know that's what it takes to be a fag. I love a fucking fag.

**Matt:** I'm not a fucking fag.

**Violet:** He was our friend! Why would — Jesus!

**Matt:** Violet — I love you. Please . . .

**Violet:** Don't come near me.

**Matt:** I knew it was wrong. I don't know why I did it. I've never done anything like that before. Never. But it doesn't mean I don't love you. I do love you. I love you more than I ever have. Right now.

**Violet:** Shut up.

**Matt:** There's gotta be some way we can work through this. I'm your husband.

**Violet:** Work through this?!

**Matt:** Understand it.

**Violet:** You're a fucking fag . . .

**Matt:** Stop saying that.

**Violet:** I can never trust you again.

**Matt:** You can . . .

**Violet:** What if you gave me AIDS?

**Matt:** He doesn't have AIDS. We didn't do anything . . .

**Violet:** Did he fuck you up the ass? Did he?!

**Matt:** No!

**Violet:** You fucked him up the ass though — didn't you?

**Matt:** It doesn't matter what we did . . .

**Violet:** You fucked him.

**Matt:** Yes I fucked him!

*Violet slaps Matt across the face, very hard.*

**Violet:** You fucking pig!

**Matt:** I can't explain it but I can stop. I'll never do it again.

**Violet:** Like I'm going to believe that.

**Matt:**  He was my friend. He wanted it. I didn't know . . .

**Violet:**  Didn't know what?

**Matt:**  Didn't know how to say no.

**Violet:**  Who are you?

**Matt:**  I know you're angry . . .

**Violet:**  You have no fucking idea how angry I am. It's all coming back and I don't know what it is except it's got something to do with men and my dad fucking off and I hate your guts right now. I hate you, Matt. Did you think about me once during this thing? If I was a man I'd kick the living shit out of you right now, Matt. I would.

**Matt:**  I didn't want to hurt you.

**Violet:**  Tell me something — don't lie to me — I mean it — don't. . . . Do you love him?

**Caption:**  Yes

**Matt:**  No.

**Violet:**  Liar.

**Matt:**  I don't.

**Violet:**  I can't believe you'd still lie to me.

**Matt:**  *Very quiet.* I love him.

**Violet:**  Cocksucking fudge packer.

**Matt:**  At least I told you. I was honest.

*Left to right:* Damian Baldet as Matt, Michael J. Blankenship as David, and Annie Fitzpatrick as Kryla. *Photo: Sandy Underwood*

**Violet:**   I want a divorce.

**Matt:**   No.

**Violet:**   You'll give me a divorce. I guarantee it.

**Matt:**   I love you too.

**Violet:**   Shut up. Give me your keys.

**Matt:**   It's not the same thing. You don't understand.

**Violet:**   Give me your keys to the apartment, Matt.

*Matt gives her the keys.*

**Violet:**   Sleep on the couch in the office until you find
a place. I'll call you after I talk to my lawyer.

**Matt:**   Don't leave me, Violet. I'm sorry.

**Violet:**   Goodbye, Matt.

*Violet exits.*

**Caption:**   Choose

*Shannon's bedroom. She is in bed sleeping. There is an IV
hooked into her arm. David sits by the bed. Shannon wakes.*

**Shannon:**   What time is it?

**David:**   Nine-thirty.

**Shannon:**   Shit myself?

**David:**   Can't smell anything.

**Shannon:**   I'll say hi to Betty Rubble for you. *[I'm going
to kill myself now]*

**David:**   No.

**Shannon:**   Yes.

**David:**   Not yet. Shan please.

**Shannon:**   I'm sick of it. Sick of sickness. Sick of using so much energy to not die that I can't live. It's time. Get out. Have a beer. Get a room. I'm going to kill myself.

**David:**   I won't let you.

**Shannon:**   You can't stop me.

**David:**   I'll use forgotten Kryptonian technology to suck the virus out of your body.

**Shannon:**   You're not Superman, David.

**David:**   Wait until the show's over.

**Shannon:**   I don't give a flying fuck about your show.

**David:**   I'll miss you too much.

**Caption:**   So Long

**Shannon:**   You have to let me go.

**Caption:**   Farewell

**Shannon:**   I don't want to be here anymore.

**Caption:**   Auf Wiedersehen

**Shannon:**   Goodbye.

*David moves to Shannon and kisses her.*

**David:**   Later, Betty.

**Shannon:**   Later.

*David exits. A light rises on Kryla in a bar.*

**Caption:**   A Bar

*David enters, seeing Kryla, who sees him.*

**Kryla:**   I didn't tell her.

**David:**   It doesn't matter.

**Kryla:**   It matters to me.

**David:**   It had nothing to do with you.

**Kryla:**   Fags think they're persecuted but they're not. Not the same way women are. Fags're still men. At least they're "men." They don't get lied to. No one tells them they'll be taken care of. No one tells them everything's gonna be all right.

**David:**   What's your point?

**Kryla:**   Everything's easy for you.

**David:**   You're an alcoholic.

**Kryla:**   You're a drug addict. And an alcoholic.

**David:**   You're bitter.

**Kryla:**   You're manipulative.

**David:**   You're more manipulative.

**Kryla:** I have to be. It's the only way we're allowed to accomplish anything.

**David:** Us too.

**Kryla:** You said you weren't sleeping with him.

**David:** It was nonna your business.

**Kryla:** Friends don't lie to each other.

**David:** Of course they do. We all lie to each other. It's what we're taught. It's how we learn to communicate.

**Kryla:** You broke up that marriage.

**David:** It would've been fine if you'd stayed out of it.

**Kryla:** A cheating husband isn't fine just because the wife doesn't know.

**David:** Matt made his own decisions.

**Kryla:** You're smarter than he is.

**David:** That gives you the right to interfere in my life?

**Kryla:** What you were doing was wrong.

**David:** Why? Because they're married?

**Kryla:** No, because he said he'd never fuck anyone else.

**David:** We all say that. And most of us mean it. For varying lengths of time.

**Kryla:**  It's not a fucking joke.

**David:**  You're a fucking joke.

**Kryla:**  You lied to me!

**David:**  You're a bitter unhappy frustrated woman!

**Kryla:**  You're a fag. You can't change that. No matter how many straight men you get involved with. You'll never be like them.

**David:**  Shut up.

**Kryla:**  You're just a fucked up kid still wanting your straight cousin or anyone like him to use you.

**David:**  Fuck you!

**Kryla:**  I'm so sick of your whining and moaning. No one understands you. You never get the breaks. All your friends are dying . . .

**David:**  Don't.

**Kryla:**  People die of other things too you know. Women die of all sorts of things. What about breast cancer?

**David:**  And just how many friends have you lost to breast cancer? This year.

**Kryla:**  Two.

**David:**  Twelve to AIDS. This year. You'll excuse me if I'm too busy to do anything but wave at the breast cancer float.

**Kryla:**  You make me sick.

**David:** Shannon's dead.

**Kryla:** What?

**David:** She's doing it right now. She's doing herself before the cancer does.

**Kryla:** Oh Jesus.

**David:** And we're standing here arguing about whose pain is the most valid.

**Kryla:** David . . . I'm sorry. . . . I'm sorry. . . .

*Kryla puts her arms around David. He remains perfectly rigid, unmoving. After a moment she lets go of him.*

**Kryla:** You have to let it out.

**David:** If I start crying now I'll never stop.

**Kryla:** Why didn't you tell me when you came in? Why didn't you stop me? Jesus, David. . . .

**David:** You're right what you said about my cousin — about straight guys — I don't know if I can change it but I want to try. I think I have to let go . . .

**Kryla:** Of me?

**David:** Of a lot things.

**Kryla:** Of me?

**David:** Yeah.

*David exits.*

**Caption:** The Final Phase

*A light rises on Shannon in bed. She is comatose. Her breathing has a harsh rattle to it.*

**Caption:** Ending Beginning

*Shannon's eyes suddenly open wide and she sits straight up in bed.*

**Shannon:** Wow!

*Shannon dies, sinking back into the bed. The light on her blinks out.*

**David:** I go to the tubs and lock myself in my room and smoke a big fat joint and think of all the guys I know who have died of AIDS so far. Murray. Sam. Jamie. Paul. Leonard. Mark. Elliot. Wendel. Ray. Tom. Brian. Geoffrey. Larry. Bob. Bill. Bernie. Russ. Harvey. Trent. Hank. Terry. Roger. John.

**Caption:** SHANNON

**David:** I can kind of see them in the dark. Their arms. Their chests. Their backs. Their asses. I can hear them whispering. I can hear water dripping from a pipe somewhere behind me. The guy in the next cubicle is snoring lightly. Peter Gabriel's singing "Salisbury Hill" on the sound system and the guy running the door's whispering into the phone. I hear the sound of a siren . . . but far away and coming closer and closer and closer.

**Caption:** The Death of Superman

*A light rises on Matt.*

**Matt:**  Superman was killed by some big guy with bones sticking out of his body, named Doomsday.

*A light rises on Violet.*

**Violet:**  Came from nowhere. No one knew anything about him.

*A light rises on Kryla.*

**Kryla:**  A nameless unknown killer with no origin and no apparent purpose except to kill Superman.

**Caption:**  Shannon Dockery
1959 to 1993

*Shannon's corpse lies in bed. David is applying make-up to Shannon's face.*

**David:**  They'll bring him back. They have to. He's Superman. But he'll be different. He won't be ours anymore.

**Caption:**  The Epitaph

*A light on Kryla writing at her computer.*

**Kryla:**  And with Superman's passing an entire generation loses the dreams of their childhood. Dreams printed on cheap paper with bright inks. Dreams of women who were constant victims and men who were impossible heroes.

**David:**  No more rules.

**Kryla:**  *To David.* The dreams of men.

**David:**  *To Kryla.* The dreams of children.

*David exits.*

**Caption:**   The Gallery

*Violet enters the gallery. She stops, staring at the paintings. Matt enters the gallery.*

**Matt:**   What are you doing here?

**Violet:**   I wanted to see them.

**Matt:**   How are you?

**Caption:**   Lie

**Violet:**   Fine.

**Caption:**   No

**Violet:**   Shitty. You're still seeing him.

**Matt:**   No. I just wanted to see them too. How's your
mom?

**Violet:**   Bitchy.

**Matt:**   The usual.

**Violet:**   Right.

**Matt:**   You . . . uh . . . seeing anyone?

**Violet:**   Not yet.

**Caption:**   The Paintings

**Violet:**   They're very good.

**Matt:**   Yeah.

**Violet:** Y'know, I almost know what you mean now?

**Matt:** What?

**Violet:** When you said it was different with him.

**Matt:** Whadaya mean?

**Violet:** They're you. But not you. Not like I knew you. Like another person with the same face and body.

**Matt:** Yeah.

**Violet:** How come he got to see that person and I never?

**Matt:** I don't know.

**Violet:** I've gotta go.

**Matt:** If you want to talk . . .

**Violet:** What was wrong with me? Didn't I love you enough? Didn't I turn you on? Was I boring? Do you think I'm ugly? When you married me you said you loved me. That you'd love me forever. Why did you lie?

**Matt:** I didn't lie. I never once didn't love you.

**Violet:** Sad.

**Matt:** Yeah.

**Violet:** He loved you as much as I did.

**Matt:** Why do you say that?

**Violet:** Take another look at those paintings, Matt.

**Caption:** Alone

*Violet exits. She moves to a spot on her own. Matt examines the paintings again. He turns, about to exit when David enters.*

**David:** This is a surprise.

**Matt:** Hi.

**David:** Glad you got to see the series all together.

**Matt:** They're great.

**David:** Yes.

**Matt:** You still mad at me?

**David:** I'm not mad at anyone anymore.

**Matt:** David, I'm so fucking lonely.

**David:** What do you need?

**Matt:** I don't know.

**Caption:** Acceptance

**Matt:** What do you need?

**David:** To understand. To change. To grow.

**Matt:** I need that too.

**David:** Good luck.

**Matt:** I still love you.

**David:** No. I don't think you do. I think you just don't like the idea of me not loving you anymore.

**Matt:** Don't you?

**Caption:** Don't Lie

**David:** I don't know.

**Matt:** Do you think we could? . . .

**David:** *Cutting him off.* I doubt it. It's too fucked up and . . . and I think — if I'm going to be with someone else — anyone else — I have to find someone like me — instead of trying to create him. It just doesn't work and I don't have the energy anymore.

**Matt:** So it's over.

*Pause.*

**David:** Yeah Matt. It's over.

**Matt:** Right.

*Matt exits to a spot on his own.*

**Caption:** Alone

*Kryla enters. She carries a comic book in a bag.*

**Kryla:** Why is it the established critics always hate your work?

**David:** Because it doesn't tell them everything's going to be all right.

**Kryla:** I think they're brilliant. *[the paintings]*

**David:** Thanks.

**Kryla:** I brought you something.

*She hands the bag to David as she speaks.*

**Kryla:**   Action Comics five hundred. The Rebirth of
Superman.

**Violet:**   Alive.

**Matt:**   Reinvented.

**Kryla:**   I thought it could be like a peace offering
maybe.

*David opens the bag and pulls out a copy of* Action Comics
#500. *He reads the cover.*

**Kryla:**   Do you still feel you have to dump everyone
you know to get where you want to go?

**David:**   I don't know.

**Kryla:**   I want to be friends again.

**David:**   It'll just be the same thing.

**Kryla:**   It doesn't have to be.

**David:**   I'm leaving Calgary.

**Kryla:**   For where?

**David:**   Toronto. Montreal. Whatever.

**Kryla:**   I'll miss you.

**David:**   We're bad for each other, Kryla. We've known
each other too long. We both need some fresh air.
Thanks for the comic, but I don't want it.

**Kryla:**   But Superman's alive.

**David:**  No. He's not.

*David hands the comic back to Kryla.*

**David:**  I've got some stuff to take care of. If you don't mind . . .

**Kryla:**  We're going to be the only two left. The only two who remember. The only two with Shannon's story or Trent's story — all the stories. I don't think I can do all that on my own and I don't think you can either. I need you, David, and I love you very much no matter what horrible, unforgivable things we have done to one another in the past or the future. Don't leave me to turn the lights out by myself pal.

*Pause. After a moment David turns to Kryla.*

**David:**  You're a fucking cow.

**Kryla:**  Thanks.

**David:**  You know just how to get me.

**Kryla:**  My mother's legacy.

**David:**  I'll send you a card. We'll talk.

**Kryla:**  I'd appreciate that.

*Kryla hands the comic back to David and exits to a spot on her own.*

**Caption:**  Alone

*David stands alone with the paintings. He looks at them, then at the comic.*

**Caption:**   Childhood

**Matt:**   Goodbye.

**Caption:**   Prince Charming

**Violet:**   Goodbye.

**Caption:**   Safety

**Kryla:**   Goodbye.

**Caption:**   Superman

*Pause. The light on Violet goes out.*

**Caption:**   Our Hero

*Pause. The light on Kryla goes out.*

**Caption:**   The Future

*Pause. The light on Matt goes out. David drops the comic book to the floor.*

**David:**   Goodbye.

**Caption:**   Beginning

*Fade to black.*

# Biography

Playwright Brad Fraser, born in Edmonton in 1959, began winning Alberta Culture Playwriting competitions when he was a seventeen-year-old student in theatre arts at Victoria Composite High School. For two summers he attended the Banff Centre Playwrights' Colony, headed by Sharon Pollock. He wrote and directed his first staged play, *Mutants*, solicited for the 1980–81 season by Walterdale Theatre Associates, Edmonton's community theatre, where he was also an actor, set designer, and stage manager. The following season, 25th Street Theatre, Saskatoon, premièred *Wolfboy*, with further productions at Theatre Network, Edmonton; Touchstone Theatre, Vancouver; and Theatre Passe Muraille, Toronto. Two other works were performed at Passe Muraille: *Rude Noises (for a Blank Generation)*, a collective creation with Paul Thompson in 1982, and *Young Art* in 1986. Fraser subsequently wrote *Chainsaw Love* (1985) and *The Return of the Bride* (1988) for the Edmonton Fringe Festival.

In 1986, Fraser became resident playwright at Edmonton's Workshop West Theatre. Here he began working on *Unidentified Human Remains and the True Nature of Love*, premièred in Calgary at Alberta Theatre Projects' play-Rites 1989. With this play Fraser achieved national and international recognition with productions in Toronto, Edmonton, Montreal, Chicago, New York, Milan, Edinburgh, London, and Tokyo. The movie version, adapted by the playwright and directed by Denys Arcand, was released in 1994. Fraser won a Genie award for the adaptation. For three seasons Fraser wrote and/or directed plays for the Edmonton Teen Festival at the Citadel Theatre: Jeffrey Hirschfield's *Blood Brothers* (1989); a revised *Young Art* (1990); and *Prom Night of the Living Dead*, with music by Darrin Hagen (1991). Release of a film version of *Prom Night* is pending. *The Ugly Man* was premièred at playRites 1992 with subsequent productions in Montreal and Edmonton. The French version, *(L'homme laid)*, directed by Derek Goldby at Théâtre de Quat'Sous, was published in spring 1993. The French translation of *Human Remains (Des restes humains non-identifiés et la véritable nature de l'amour)* was published in 1993.

Fraser is currently working for the Walt Disney Corporation, Touchstone Division, on a feature film titled *Beauty,* and writing a film called *Our Man in Manila* for Alliance. Negotiations are in process to develop a late night soap opera for Showtime. Fraser's next stage project is a musical version of the Craig Russell movie, *Outrageous,* in collaboration with Darrin Hagen and Andy Northrup. *Time* magazine recently named *Poor Super Man* one of the top ten plays of 1994.